Happy Birthday Claire!
Thought this may
come in handy in your
new island home-cabuan.

With love-
Annette

fish

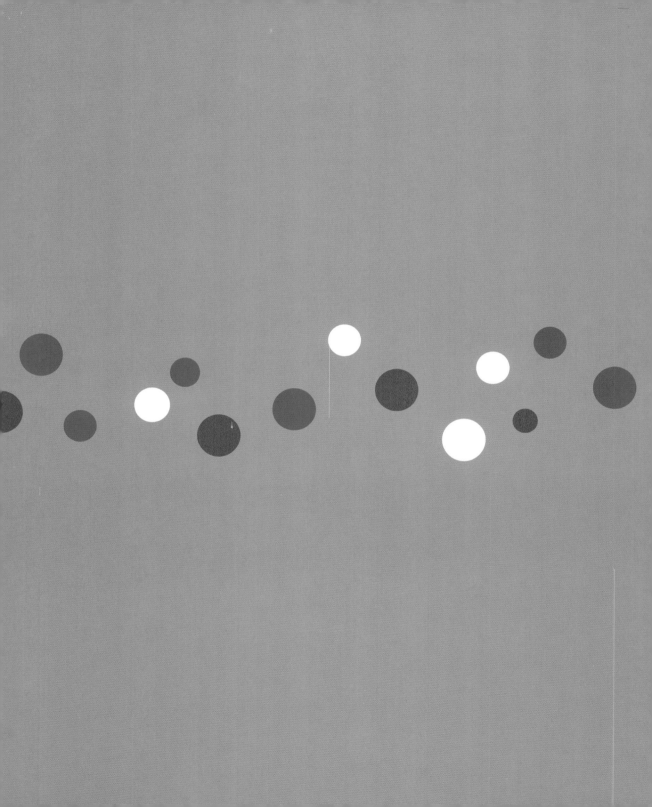

fish

MURDOCH BOOKS

contents

fishy tales

With around 71 per cent of the world's surface covered by water, it is little wonder that fish life abounds. One of our most important sources of protein, fish come in a head-spinning array of sizes, shapes and colours. We make use of all sorts of fish for culinary purposes — from behemoths like tuna, moonfish or swordfish, to tiddlers such as anchovies, whitebait and sardines. Fish is amazingly versatile and can be cooked in a plethora of ways — from steaming, poaching and baking whole to grilling and shallow- or deep-frying. In fact, some ultra-fresh specimens can even be sliced and served raw.

The various species of other seafood come under the general heading 'fish' for the purposes of this book too. And what similarly scrumptious critters are found in their ranks! From the luxury of prawns (shrimp), scallops, lobsters and crabs to more prosaic creatures like mussels, squid and octopus, the bounty of the sea makes a worthy feast, whatever the occasion. All of the world's great cuisines make a feature of fish and seafood, so the repertoire of fishy recipes runs deep.

Fish is easy to cook, although some are intimidated by the prospect. The best course of action is to find a good fishmonger or market, where there'll be some obliging soul on hand to gut, fillet and skin fresh fish for you. Buy from the experts and you'll be confident of freshness and quality too. Then all that's left is to cook and enjoy!

pot

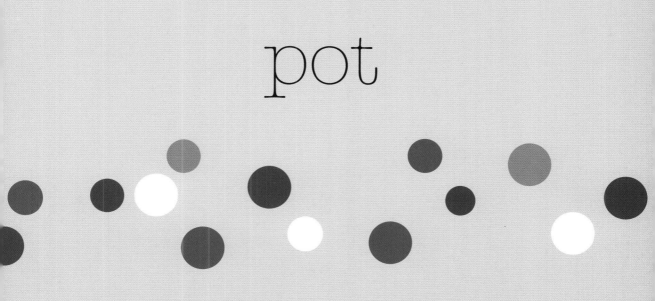

Moules marinières

50 g (1¾ oz) butter
1 large onion, chopped
½ celery stalk, chopped
2 garlic cloves, crushed
400 ml (14 fl oz) dry white wine
1 bay leaf
2 thyme sprigs
2 kg (4 lb 8 oz) black mussels,
   cleaned and 'beards' removed
230 ml (7¾ fl oz) thick (double/heavy) cream
2 tablespoons chopped flat-leaf (Italian) parsley

Melt the butter in a large saucepan over medium heat. Add the onion, celery and garlic and cook, stirring occasionally, for about 5 minutes, or until the onion is softened but not browned.

Add the wine, bay leaf and thyme to the saucepan and bring to the boil. Add the mussels, cover the pan tightly and simmer over low heat for 2–3 minutes, shaking the pan occasionally. Use tongs to lift out the mussels as they open and put them into a warm dish. Discard any mussels that have not opened.

Strain the liquid through a fine sieve lined with muslin (cheesecloth) into a clean saucepan, to get rid of any grit or sand. Bring to the boil and boil for 2 minutes. Add the cream and reheat the sauce without boiling. Season well. Serve the mussels in individual bowls with the liquid poured over. Sprinkle with the parsley and serve with plenty of bread.

SERVES 6 AS A STARTER

Spaghetti marinara

1 tablespoon olive oil
1 onion, chopped
3 garlic cloves, crushed
2 x 400 g (14 oz) tins crushed
   tomatoes
2 tablespoons tomato paste
   (concentrated purée)
170 ml (5½ fl oz/⅔ cup) dry
   white wine
2 teaspoons soft brown sugar
1 teaspoon finely grated
   lemon zest
2 tablespoons chopped basil

12 raw medium prawns
   (shrimp), peeled and
   deveined
12 large scallops, without roe,
   membrane removed
2 small squid tubes (300 g/
   10½ oz), cleaned and cut into
   1 cm (½ inch) rings
300 g (10½ oz) spaghetti
2 tablespoons finely chopped
   flat-leaf (Italian) parsley
shaved parmesan cheese,
   to serve

Heat the oil in a large saucepan, add the onion and cook over medium heat for 5–8 minutes, or until golden. Add the garlic, tomato, tomato paste, wine, sugar, lemon zest, half the basil and 250 ml (9 fl oz/1 cup) water. Cook for 1 hour, stirring occasionally, or until the sauce is reduced and thickened. Season with salt and ground black pepper.

Add the prawns to the pan and cook for 1 minute, then add the scallops and cook for 2 minutes. Stir in the squid and cook for 1 minute more, or until all of the seafood is cooked through and tender.

Meanwhile, cook the spaghetti in a large saucepan of boiling water until *al dente*. Drain and toss with the sauce, parsley and remaining basil. Serve topped with shavings of parmesan cheese.

SERVES 4

Fish molee

1 tablespoon oil
1 large onion, thinly sliced
3 garlic cloves, crushed
1–2 small green chillies, finely chopped
2 teaspoons ground turmeric
1 teaspoon ground coriander
1 teaspoon ground cumin
4 cloves
6 curry leaves, plus another 6 to garnish
800 ml (28 fl oz) coconut milk
500 g (1 lb 2 oz) skinless pomfret or flounder fillets
1 tablespoon chopped coriander (cilantro) leaves

Heat the oil in a large, wide saucepan or sauté pan and cook the onion for 5 minutes. Add the garlic and chilli and cook for a further 5 minutes, or until the onion has softened and looks translucent. Add the turmeric, ground coriander, cumin and cloves and stir-fry with the onion for about 2 minutes before stirring in the curry leaves, coconut milk and ½ teaspoon salt. Bring to just below boiling point. Reduce the heat to medium and simmer, without a lid, for 20 minutes, or until slightly thickened.

Cut each fish fillet into two or three large pieces across the fillet. Add the fish to the sauce and bring the sauce back to a simmer, then cook for 5 minutes or until the fish is opaque and looks flaky. Season with a little more salt if necessary, then stir in the fresh coriander leaves. Serve garnished with curry leaves. Serve with boiled rice to soak up the sauce.

SERVES 4

Thai prawn curry

Curry paste

1 small onion, roughly chopped

3 garlic cloves

4 dried red chillies

4 whole black peppercorns

2 tablespoons chopped
lemongrass, white part only

1 tablespoon chopped coriander
(cilantro) root

2 teaspoons grated lime zest

2 teaspoons cumin seeds

1 teaspoon sweet paprika

1 teaspoon ground coriander

2 tablespoons oil

1 tablespoon oil

2 tablespoons fish sauce

2 cm (¾ inch) piece fresh
galangal, thinly sliced

4 makrut (kaffir lime) leaves

400 ml (14 fl oz) coconut cream

1 kg (2 lb 4 oz) raw medium
prawns (shrimp), peeled and
deveined, tails intact

sliced red chillies, to garnish
(optional)

coriander (cilantro) leaves,
to garnish

To make the curry paste, put the onion, garlic, dried chillies, peppercorns, lemongrass, coriander root, lime zest, cumin, paprika, ground coriander, 2 tablespoons oil and 1 teaspoon salt in a small food processor. Whiz until the mixture forms a smooth paste.

Heat the oil in a large saucepan. Add half the curry paste (refrigerate the rest for next time) and stir over low heat for 30 seconds. Add the fish sauce, galangal, lime leaves and coconut cream to the pan and stir until well combined.

Add the prawns to the pan and simmer, uncovered, for 10 minutes, or until the prawns are cooked and the sauce has thickened slightly. Sprinkle with chilli, if using, and coriander leaves and serve with steamed rice.

SERVES 4

Brazilian seafood stew

4 x 200 g (7 oz) white fish steaks
200 g (7 oz) raw large prawns
    (shrimp), peeled and deveined
2½ tablespoons lime juice
2 tablespoons olive oil
1 large onion, finely chopped
4 large garlic cloves, crushed
1 large red capsicum (pepper),
    chopped

1 habañero chilli, seeded and
    finely chopped
500 g (1 lb 2 oz) ripe tomatoes
300 ml (10½ fl oz) coconut milk
chopped coriander (cilantro)
    leaves, to garnish
thin strips of lime zest, to
    garnish

Put the fish and prawns in a shallow non-metallic dish. Drizzle the lime juice over the top, season, then turn the seafood in the juice. Cover and marinate in the fridge for 30 minutes.

Meanwhile, heat the oil in a large saucepan and add the onion. Cook for about 10 minutes, or until softened, then add the garlic, capsicum and chilli and cook for a further 3 minutes, stirring now and then.

Score a cross in the base of each tomato. Soak in boiling water for 30 seconds, then plunge into cold water. Drain and peel the skin away from the cross. Chop the tomatoes, discarding the cores.

Add the tomatoes to the pan and cook for 5 minutes, or until the mixture thickens. Allow to cool a little, then tip the mixture into a food processor or blender and blend until smooth. Return the sauce to the pan. Pour in the coconut milk and bring to a gentle simmer. Lift the fish and prawns out of the marinating dish and add to the pan, leaving behind any remaining marinade. Cook for 4 minutes, or until cooked. Season and sprinkle with coriander and lime zest.

SERVES 4

Greek octopus in red wine stew

1 kg (2 lb 4 oz) baby octopus
2 tablespoons olive oil
1 large onion, chopped
3 garlic cloves, crushed
1 bay leaf
750 ml (26 fl oz/3 cups) red wine
3 tablespoons red wine vinegar
400 g (14 oz) tin crushed
  tomatoes
1 tablespoon tomato paste
  (concentrated purée)
1 tablespoon chopped oregano
¼ teaspoon ground cinnamon
small pinch ground cloves
1 teaspoon sugar
2 tablespoons finely chopped
  flat-leaf (Italian) parsley

Cut between the head and tentacles of the octopus, just below the eyes. Grasp the body and push the beak out and up through the centre of the tentacles with your fingers. Cut the eyes from the head by slicing a small disc off. Discard the eye section. Carefully slit through one side, avoiding the ink sac, and scrape out any gut. Rinse the octopus well under running water.

Heat the oil in a large saucepan, add the onion and cook over medium heat for 5 minutes, or until starting to brown. Add the garlic and bay leaf and cook for another minute. Add the octopus and stir to coat in the onion mixture.

Stir in the wine, vinegar, tomatoes, tomato paste, oregano, cinnamon, cloves and sugar. Bring to the boil, then reduce the heat and simmer for 1 hour, or until the octopus is tender and the sauce has thickened slightly. Stir in the parsley and season to taste with salt and ground black pepper. Serve with a Greek salad and some crusty bread to mop up the juices.

SERVES 4–6

Penang laksa

800 g (1 lb 12 oz) whole snapper, scaled and gutted

3 tablespoons tamarind purée

1 teaspoon soft brown sugar

1 tablespoon oil

125 g (4½ oz) thin dried white rice noodles, soaked in boiling water for 10 minutes

100 g (3½ oz) piece cucumber, peeled and cut into thin batons

2 red Asian shallots, thinly sliced

200 g (7 oz) pineapple, cut into small chunks

1 small red chilli, sliced (optional)

25 g (1 oz) Vietnamese mint, small leaves left whole, the rest roughly shredded

Curry paste

1 small onion

1 teaspoon chopped fresh turmeric

1 tablespoon grated fresh ginger

2 small red chillies, roughly chopped

1 teaspoon shrimp paste

Put the fish in a large saucepan and cover with cold water. Add 1 teaspoon salt and bring to the boil. Cook for 10 minutes, skimming off any scum. Lift out the fish. Drain the liquid, reserving 750 ml (26 fl oz/3 cups) in the pan, then add the tamarind and sugar. Take the fish off the bone, discarding the head and skin. Flake roughly.

To make the curry paste, put all the ingredients and 2 tablespoons water in a food processor and briefly whiz into a paste.

Heat the oil in a large saucepan and add the curry paste. Cook for 5 minutes, stirring constantly. Pour in the reserved liquid, bring to the boil, then reduce to a simmer for 5 minutes. Add the fish just for long enough to heat through.

Divide the noodles among four deep bowls. Top with the remaining ingredients. Ladle the soup into the bowls, then serve.

SERVES 4

Seafood risotto

1.75 litres (60 fl oz/7 cups) fish stock
2 tablespoons olive oil
2 onions, finely chopped
2 garlic cloves, finely chopped
1 celery stalk, finely chopped
440 g (15½ oz/2 cups) risotto rice
8–10 black mussels, cleaned and 'beards' removed

150 g (5½ oz) skinless blue-eye or cod fillet, cut into bite-sized pieces
8 raw large prawns (shrimp), peeled and deveined, tails intact
2 tablespoons chopped flat-leaf (Italian) parsley
2 tablespoons chopped oregano

Bring the stock to the boil in a saucepan. Reduce until just simmering, then cover.

Heat the oil in a large saucepan over medium heat. Add the onion, garlic and celery and cook for 2–3 minutes. Add 2 tablespoons water, cover and cook for 5 minutes, or until the vegetables soften. Add the rice and cook, stirring, for 3–4 minutes, or until the rice grains are well coated.

Gradually add 125 ml (4 fl oz/½ cup) of the hot stock to the rice, stirring over low heat with a wooden spoon until all the stock has been absorbed. Repeat, adding 125 ml (4 fl oz/½ cup) stock each time until only a small amount of stock is left and the rice is just tender — this should take 20–25 minutes.

Meanwhile, bring 3 tablespoons water to the boil in a saucepan. Add the mussels, cover with a lid and cook for 4–5 minutes, shaking the pan occasionally, until the mussels have opened. Drain and discard any mussels that have not opened. Set aside.

Stir the fish, prawns and remaining stock into the rice. Cook for about 7 minutes, or until the seafood is just cooked and the rice is tender. Add the mussels, cover and set aside off the heat for 5 minutes. Stir in the herbs, then season. Rest before serving.

SERVES 4

Tagliatelle with prawns and cream

500 g (1 lb 2 oz) fresh tagliatelle
60 g (2¼ oz) butter
6 spring onions (scallions), finely chopped
500 g (1 lb 2 oz) raw medium prawns (shrimp),
    peeled and deveined, tails intact
3 tablespoons brandy
300 ml (10½ fl oz) thick (double/heavy) cream
1 tablespoon chopped thyme
4 tablespoons chopped flat-leaf (Italian) parsley

Cook the pasta in a large saucepan of boiling water until *al dente*. Drain well.

Meanwhile, melt the butter in a large heavy-based saucepan, add the spring onion and stir for 2 minutes. Add the prawns and stir for 2 minutes, or until they just start to change colour. Remove the prawns from the pan and set aside.

Splash in the brandy and boil for 2 minutes, or until the brandy is reduced by half. Stir in the cream, then add the thyme and half the parsley. Season with freshly ground black pepper. Simmer for 5 minutes, or until the sauce begins to thicken. Return the prawns to the sauce and cook for 2 minutes. Season well.

Toss the sauce through the pasta. If you prefer a thinner sauce, add a little hot water or milk. Sprinkle with the remaining parsley, then serve.

SERVES 4

Creamy cod stew

3 ripe tomatoes
1 tablespoon dried shrimp
3 tablespoons olive oil
1 onion, chopped
1 small green capsicum
   (pepper), chopped
1 small green chilli, finely
   chopped
3 garlic cloves, crushed
3 tablespoons crunchy peanut
   butter

400 ml (14 fl oz) coconut milk
100 g (3½ oz) small okra,
   topped and tailed
½ teaspoon paprika
600 g (1 lb 5 oz) skinless cod
   fillets
3 tablespoons coriander
   (cilantro) leaves

Score a cross in the base of each tomato. Soak in boiling water for 30 seconds, then plunge into cold water. Drain and peel the skin away from the cross. Chop the tomatoes, discarding the cores and seeds and reserving any juices. Put the dried shrimp in a small bowl, cover with boiling water and leave to soak for 10 minutes, then drain.

Heat the oil in a large, wide saucepan or sauté pan. Add the onion and capsicum and cook for 5 minutes, stirring occasionally. Add the chilli and garlic and cook for a further 2 minutes. Add the tomatoes and juices, peanut butter, coconut milk, okra, paprika and dried shrimp. Bring the mixture to the boil, then reduce the heat to medium and simmer for 12–15 minutes, or until the okra are tender.

Meanwhile, cut the cod into large chunks.

Add the fish to the pan, stir and simmer gently to cook. Test after 3 minutes — if the cod flakes easily, it is ready. Season and scatter the coriander over the top.

SERVES 4

Tomato and basil black mussels

125 ml (4 fl oz/½ cup) dry white wine
2 bay leaves
1 kg (2 lb 4 oz) black mussels, cleaned and 'beards' removed
500 g (1 lb 2 oz/2 cups) tomato pasta sauce
1–2 teaspoons sugar, to taste
2 tablespoons extra virgin olive oil
4 tablespoons shredded basil
2 tablespoons snipped chives

Place the wine and bay leaves in a large, wide saucepan and bring to the boil. Add the mussels to the saucepan and cook, covered with a tight-fitting lid, over high heat for 4 minutes, or until the mussels open.

Meanwhile, place the pasta sauce, sugar, oil and basil in a bowl and mix well.

Discard any mussels that have not opened. Drain, reserving the cooking juices. Return the mussels to the saucepan, add the tomato mixture and 125 ml (4 fl oz/½ cup) of the reserved cooking juices and stir over high heat for 3–4 minutes, or until warmed through. Sprinkle with chives and serve in warmed bowls with bread.

SERVES 4 AS A STARTER

Light red seafood curry

Chu chee paste

10 large dried red chillies

1 tablespoon shrimp paste

1 tablespoon white peppercorns

1 teaspoon coriander seeds

2 teaspoons finely grated makrut (kaffir lime) zest

10 makrut (kaffir lime) leaves, finely shredded

1 tablespoon chopped coriander (cilantro) stem

1 lemongrass stem, white part only, finely chopped

3 tablespoons chopped fresh galangal

6 garlic cloves, chopped

10 red Asian shallots, chopped

2 x 270 ml (9½ fl oz) tins coconut milk

500 g (1 lb 2 oz) raw large prawns (shrimp), peeled and deveined, tails intact

500 g (1 lb 2 oz) scallops, without roe, membrane removed

2 tablespoons fish sauce

2 tablespoons soft brown sugar

8 makrut (kaffir lime) leaves, finely shredded

1 large handful Thai basil

Preheat the oven to 180°C (350°F/Gas 4). Soak the chillies in hot water for 15 minutes. Drain, remove the seeds and chop the flesh. Put the shrimp paste, peppercorns and coriander seeds on a foil-lined baking tray and bake for 5 minutes. Blend the baked spices in a food processor with the remaining paste ingredients until smooth.

Remove 250 ml (9 fl oz/1 cup) thick coconut cream from the top of the tins (reserve the rest) and place in a large, wide saucepan or wok. Heat until just boiling, then stir in 3 tablespoons of the curry paste. Reduce the heat. Simmer for 10 minutes, or until the mixture is fragrant and the oil begins to separate. Stir in the seafood and remaining coconut milk and cook for 5 minutes. Add the fish sauce, sugar and lime leaves and cook for 1 minute. Stir in half the basil and use the rest to garnish.

SERVES 4

Caldeirada

800 g (1 lb 12 oz) boiling potatoes, cut into thick slices
3 tablespoons olive oil
1 large onion, thinly sliced
4 large garlic cloves, finely chopped
1 red capsicum (pepper), sliced
1 tablespoon paprika
1 tablespoon red wine vinegar
100 ml (3½ fl oz) dry white wine
400 g (14 oz) black mussels, cleaned and 'beards' removed
4 x 100 g (3½ oz) hake, cod or bream steaks
12 raw medium prawns (shrimp), peeled and deveined

Put the potato slices in a saucepan, cover with boiling water, then bring to the boil. Reduce the heat to medium, add a pinch of salt and simmer for 10 minutes, or until tender. Drain and arrange in a serving dish, keeping warm in a low oven if necessary.

Meanwhile, heat the oil in a large, wide saucepan or sauté pan and cook the onion for 5 minutes over medium heat. Add the garlic and capsicum and cook for a minute, stirring. Add the paprika, vinegar, wine and 2½ tablespoons water. Bring to the boil, add the mussels and cover. Allow to bubble for 4 minutes (the mussels should open), then remove the mussels from the pan, discarding any that have not opened. Reduce the heat to low.

Put the fish steaks and prawns on top of the onion mixture, cover and cook for 7 minutes, turning both once during cooking. Return the mussels to the pan for the final minute to heat through. When cooked the fish will be opaque and the prawns will be pink. Season. Spoon the seafood mixture over the top of the potato, then serve.

SERVES 4

Hot and sour fish stew

Spice paste

2 lemongrass stems, white part
   only, each cut into three
   pieces
1 teaspoon ground turmeric
small knob of fresh galangal or
   ginger
3 small red chillies
1 large garlic clove
4 red Asian shallots
1 teaspoon shrimp paste

3 tablespoons oil
½ small red capsicum (pepper),
   thinly sliced

3 tablespoons tamarind purée
   or lemon juice
1 tablespoon fish sauce
2 teaspoons grated palm sugar
   (jaggery) or soft brown sugar
225 g (8 oz) tin sliced bamboo
   shoots, drained
500 g (1 lb 2 oz) skinless
   pomfret, lemon sole or plaice
   fillets, cut into bite-sized
   pieces
2 tablespoons chopped
   coriander (cilantro) leaves
1 tablespoon chopped mint

To make the spice paste, put all the ingredients in a small food processor and process to a paste. Alternatively, finely chop all the ingredients with a knife and mix them together by hand.

Heat the oil in a large saucepan, then add the paste. Cook for 10 minutes, stirring. Add the strips of capsicum and cook for a further minute. Pour in 750 ml (26 fl oz/ 3 cups) water, the tamarind, fish sauce, sugar and ½ teaspoon salt and bring to the boil. Reduce the heat to low and simmer for 5 minutes, then add the bamboo shoots and fish pieces and poach the fish gently for 3–4 minutes, or until opaque. Stir in the coriander and mint and serve with plenty of rice.

SERVES 4

Steamed clams with corn and bacon

25 g (1 oz) butter
1 large onion, chopped
100 g (3½ oz) bacon, chopped
1.5 kg (3 lb 5 oz) clams (vongole), cleaned
1 large corn cob, kernels removed
150 ml (5 fl oz) alcoholic dry cider
150 ml (5 fl oz) thick (double/heavy) cream

Melt the butter in a large saucepan and, when hot, add the onion and bacon. Cook over medium heat for about 5 minutes, or until the onion is soft and the bacon is cooked.

Put the clams in a large saucepan with 3 tablespoons water and place over medium–high heat. Once the water is hot and the clams begin to steam, cover with a lid and cook for 2–3 minutes, or until they open. Discard any that have not opened. Strain the liquid through a sieve lined with muslin (cheesecloth) and reserve.

Add the corn kernels to the onion and bacon and cook, stirring, for 3–4 minutes, or until tender. Pour in the cider and 3 tablespoons of the reserved clam cooking liquid. Bring to the boil, then simmer for 2 minutes. Stir in the cream, and season with salt and ground black pepper. Tip in the clams and toss them in the sauce. Serve in warmed deep bowls.

SERVES 4

New England clam chowder

1.5 kg (3 lb 5 oz) clams
  (vongole), cleaned
2 teaspoons olive oil
3 bacon slices, chopped
1 onion, chopped
1 garlic clove, crushed
750 g (1 lb 10 oz) all-purpose
  potatoes, diced

330 ml (11¼ fl oz/1⅓ cups) fish
  stock
500 ml (17 fl oz/2 cups) milk
125 ml (4 fl oz/½ cup) pouring
  (whipping) cream
3 tablespoons chopped flat-leaf
  (Italian) parsley

Put the clams in a large heavy-based saucepan with 250 ml (9 fl oz/1 cup) water, cover and simmer for about 4 minutes, or until they open. Discard any that have not opened. Strain the liquid through a sieve lined with muslin (cheesecloth) and reserve. Pull most of the clams out of their shells, leaving a few intact.

Heat the oil in the cleaned saucepan. Add the bacon, onion and garlic and cook, stirring, over medium heat until the onion is soft and the bacon golden. Add the potato and stir well.

Add enough water to the reserved clam liquid to make 330 ml (11¼ fl oz/1⅓ cups) of liquid in total. Pour this and the stock into the saucepan and bring to the boil, then pour in the milk and bring back to the boil. Reduce the heat, cover and simmer for 20 minutes, or until the potato is tender. Uncover and simmer for 10 minutes, or until slightly thickened. Add the cream, clam meat and parsley and season. Heat through gently, but do not allow to boil or it may curdle. Serve in deep bowls with the clams in shells on the top.

SERVES 4

Malaysian fish curry

4 red chillies, roughly chopped, plus extra, sliced, to garnish
1 onion, chopped
4 garlic cloves
3 lemongrass stems, white part only, sliced
4 cm (1½ inch) piece of fresh ginger, sliced
2 teaspoons shrimp paste
3 tablespoons oil
1 tablespoon fish curry powder (see Note)

250 ml (9 fl oz/1 cup) coconut milk
1 tablespoon tamarind concentrate
1 tablespoon kecap manis
500 g (1 lb 2 oz) skinless ling or flake fillets, cut into bite-sized pieces
2 ripe tomatoes, chopped
1 tablespoon lemon juice
coriander (cilantro) leaves, to garnish

Combine the chilli, onion, garlic, lemongrass, ginger and shrimp paste in a small food processor and process until roughly chopped. Add 2 tablespoons of the oil and process until the mixture forms a smooth paste, regularly scraping down the side of the bowl with a spatula.

Heat the remaining oil in a large, wide saucepan or wok and add the paste. Cook for 3–4 minutes over low heat, stirring constantly, until very fragrant. Add the curry powder and stir for another 2 minutes. Add the coconut milk, tamarind, kecap manis and 250 ml (9 fl oz/1 cup) water to the pan. Bring to the boil, stirring occasionally, then reduce the heat and simmer for 10 minutes, or until slightly thickened.

Add the fish, tomato and lemon juice. Season to taste. Simmer for 5 minutes, or until the fish is just cooked. Garnish with chilli and coriander and serve with rice.

SERVES 4

NOTE: Fish curry powder is available from Asian food stores.

Prawn gumbo

2 tablespoons olive oil
1 large onion, finely chopped
3 garlic cloves, crushed
1 red capsicum (pepper), chopped
4 bacon slices, chopped
1½ teaspoons dried thyme
2 teaspoons dried oregano
1 teaspoon paprika
½ teaspoon cayenne pepper
3 tablespoons sherry
1 litre (35 fl oz/4 cups) fish stock
100 g (3½ oz/½ cup) long-grain rice
2 bay leaves
400 g (14 oz) tin chopped tomatoes
150 g (5½ oz) okra, thinly sliced
850 g (1 lb 14 oz) raw medium prawns (shrimp),
    peeled and deveined
3 tablespoons finely chopped flat-leaf (Italian) parsley

Heat the oil in a large saucepan over low heat. Cook the onion, garlic, capsicum and bacon for 5 minutes, or until soft. Stir in the herbs and spices. Season. Add the sherry and cook until evaporated, then add the stock and 500 ml (17 fl oz/2 cups) water. Bring to the boil. Add the rice and bay leaves, reduce the heat and simmer, covered, for 20 minutes.

Add the tomato and okra. Simmer, covered, for 20–25 minutes. Stir in the prawns and parsley and simmer for 5 minutes, or until the prawns are cooked through.

SERVES 4

Russian fish soup

50 g (1¾ oz) butter
1 large onion, thinly sliced
1 celery stalk, chopped
5 tablespoons plain (all-purpose) flour
2 tablespoons tomato paste (concentrated purée)
1 litre (35 fl oz/4 cups) fish stock
2 large gherkins (pickles), rinsed and chopped
1 tablespoon capers, rinsed and squeezed dry
1 bay leaf
¼ teaspoon freshly grated nutmeg
600 g (1 lb 5 oz) skinless mixed carp, perch or bream fillets,
    cut into bite-sized pieces
2 tablespoons chopped flat-leaf (Italian) parsley
2 tablespoons chopped dill, plus a little extra, to garnish
sour cream, to serve

Melt the butter in a large saucepan. Add the onion and celery and cook gently over low heat for 7–8 minutes, or until softened and translucent. Increase the heat, stir in the flour and tomato paste and cook, stirring constantly, for 30 seconds. Pour in the fish stock and slowly bring to the boil, stirring frequently.

Reduce the heat to low and add the gherkins, capers, bay leaf, nutmeg and pieces of fish. Poach gently for 2–3 minutes, or until the fish is opaque. Gently stir in the parsley and dill and season generously with salt and pepper. Serve each bowlful of soup topped with a spoonful of sour cream and a sprinkling of dill.

SERVES 4

Cioppino

2 whole crabs
3 tablespoons olive oil
1 large onion, finely chopped
1 carrot, finely chopped
2–3 garlic cloves, crushed
1 red chilli, finely chopped
400 g (14 oz) tin chopped
   tomatoes
1 tablespoon tomato paste
   (concentrated purée)
250 ml (9 fl oz/1 cup) red wine
500 ml (17 fl oz/2 cups) fish stock
1 thyme sprig

2 flat-leaf (Italian) parsley sprigs
375 g (13 oz) raw medium
   prawns (shrimp), peeled and
   deveined
1 kg (2 lb 4 oz) skinless mixed
   hake, snapper or monkfish
   fillets, cut into bite-sized
   pieces
12–15 black mussels, cleaned
   and 'beards' removed
1 tablespoon chopped flat-leaf
   (Italian) parsley, extra
1 tablespoon chopped basil

Pull the apron back from underneath the crab and separate the shells. Remove the feathery gills and intestines. Twist off the claws. Using a cleaver or large, heavy knife, cut the crabs into quarters. Crack the claws either with crab crackers or the back of a heavy knife.

Heat the oil in a large heavy-based saucepan, add the onion, carrot, garlic and chilli and stir over medium heat for about 5 minutes, or until the onion is soft. Add the tomatoes, tomato paste, wine, stock, thyme and parsley sprigs. Bring to the boil, reduce the heat, then cover and simmer for 30 minutes.

Add the crab pieces to the broth and simmer for 5 minutes, then add the prawns and simmer for 1 minute. Add the fish pieces and mussels and simmer for another 2–3 minutes, or until the fish pieces are opaque. Season well. Discard any mussels that have not opened. Sprinkle with parsley and basil before serving.

SERVES 4

Hot and sour
prawn soup

1 kg (2 lb 4 oz) raw medium prawns (shrimp)
1 tablespoon oil
2 tablespoons tom yum paste
2 lemongrass stems, white part only, bruised
4 makrut (kaffir lime) leaves
3 small red chillies, thinly sliced
4–5 tablespoons fish sauce
4–5 tablespoons lime juice
2 teaspoons grated palm sugar (jaggery) or soft brown sugar
4 spring onions (scallions), thinly sliced on the diagonal
4 tablespoons coriander (cilantro) leaves

Peel and devein the prawns, leaving the tails intact. Reserve the prawn shells and heads. Cover the prawns and refrigerate.

Heat a large, wide saucepan or wok over high heat, add the oil and swirl to coat. Cook the prawn shells and heads over medium heat for 8–10 minutes, or until they turn orange.

Add the tom yum paste and 3 tablespoons water and cook for 1 minute, or until fragrant. Add 2.25 litres (79 fl oz/9 cups) water, bring to the boil, then reduce the heat and simmer for 20 minutes. Strain into a large bowl, discarding the prawn shells and heads. Return the stock to the pan.

Add the prawns, lemongrass, lime leaves and chilli and simmer for 4–5 minutes, or until the prawns are cooked. Stir in the fish sauce, lime juice, sugar, spring onion and coriander. Discard the lemongrass and serve immediately.

SERVES 4

Red emperor poached in coconut milk

1 litre (35 fl oz/4 cups) coconut milk

2 teaspoons grated fresh ginger

3 small red chillies, finely chopped

1 tablespoon chopped coriander (cilantro) roots and stems

6 red Asian shallots, finely chopped

6 makrut (kaffir lime) leaves, shredded

2 lemongrass stems, white part only, sliced

2 teaspoons grated lime zest

500 ml (17 fl oz/2 cups) fish stock

4 tablespoons fish sauce

4 tablespoons lime juice, strained

4 x 250 g (9 oz) skinless red emperor fillets, each fillet cut into three equal portions

coriander (cilantro) leaves, to garnish

1 small red chilli, sliced, to garnish

2 makrut (kaffir lime) leaves, extra, shredded, to garnish

Bring the coconut milk to the boil in a saucepan and boil for 3 minutes. Add the ginger, chilli, coriander roots and stems, chopped shallots, lime leaves, lemongrass and lime zest and bring back to the boil. Add the fish stock and fish sauce and simmer for 15 minutes. Pass through a fine strainer and add the lime juice. Taste and add extra fish sauce if necessary.

Heat the sauce in a large, wide saucepan or wok. When it comes to the boil, add the fish, then reduce the heat and simmer gently for 10 minutes, or until cooked.

Carefully transfer the fish to a serving platter. Serve with some of the liquid and a sprinkling of coriander, chilli and shreds of lime leaf.

SERVES 4

Prawn jambalaya

1 kg (2 lb 4 oz) raw large
   prawns (shrimp), peeled
   and deveined, heads, shells
   and tails reserved
2 small onions, chopped
2 celery stalks, chopped
250 ml (9 fl oz/1 cup) dry white
   wine
3 tablespoons olive oil
200 g (7 oz) chorizo or spicy
   sausage, chopped

1 red capsicum (pepper),
   chopped
400 g (14 oz) tin chopped
   tomatoes
½ teaspoon cayenne pepper
¼ teaspoon dried thyme
¼ teaspoon dried oregano
400 g (14 oz/2 cups) long-grain
   rice

Put the prawn heads, shells and tails in a large saucepan with half of the onion, half the celery, the wine and 1 litre (35 fl oz/4 cups) water. Bring to the boil, then reduce the heat and simmer for 20 minutes. Strain through a fine sieve, reserving the prawn stock.

Heat the oil in a large, wide saucepan and cook the sausage for 5 minutes, or until browned. Remove from the pan with a slotted spoon and set aside.

Add the remaining onion and celery, and the red capsicum to the pan and cook, stirring occasionally, for 5 minutes. Add the tomatoes, cayenne pepper, dried herbs and ½ teaspoon freshly ground black pepper and bring to the boil. Reduce the heat and simmer, covered, for 10 minutes. Return the sausage to the pan and add the rice and prawn stock. Bring back to the boil, reduce the heat and simmer, covered, for 25 minutes, or until almost all the liquid has been absorbed and the rice is tender. Add the prawns and stir through gently. Cover and cook for another 5 minutes, or until the prawns are pink and cooked through.

SERVES 6

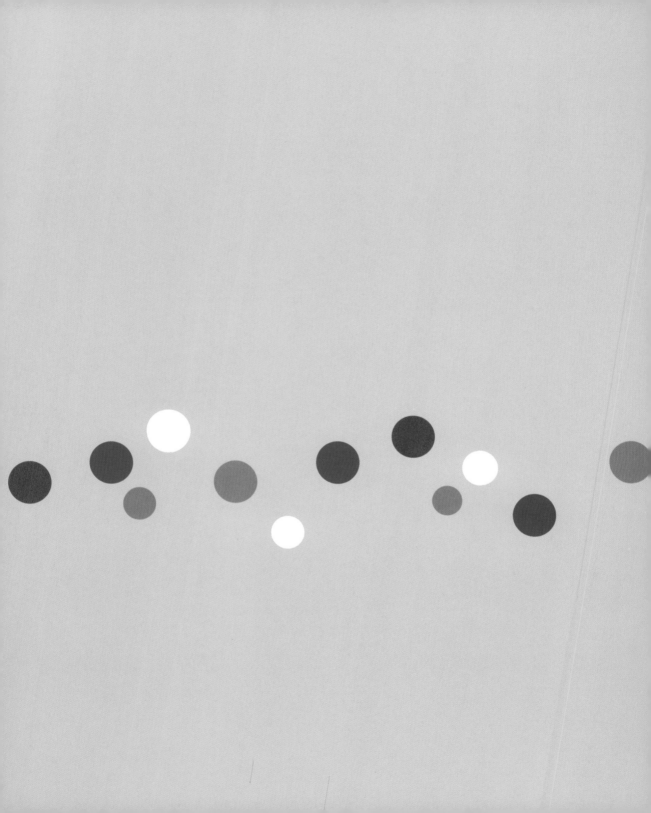

pan

Saffron fish cakes with herbed crème fraîche

160 ml (5¼ fl oz) milk
2 pinches saffron threads
500 g (1 lb 2 oz) skinless firm
   white fish fillets
4 large all-purpose potatoes, cut
   into chunks
2 garlic cloves, unpeeled
2 tablespoons plain (all-purpose)
   flour
2 teaspoons grated lemon zest

1 handful flat-leaf (Italian)
   parsley, finely chopped
2 tablespoons pouring
   (whipping) cream
4 tablespoons crème fraîche
2 tablespoons finely chopped
   mint
2 tablespoons finely chopped
   flat-leaf (Italian) parsley, extra
20–40 g (¾–1½ oz) butter

Put the milk and saffron in a frying pan and heat until simmering. Add the fish, turn up the heat a little and cook until the fish turns opaque and flaky — you might need to turn it over halfway through. Don't worry if it breaks up. Lift the fish out of the milk into a bowl and break it up roughly with a fork. Keep the milk.

Cook the potato and garlic in simmering water for about 12 minutes, or until the potato is tender. Drain the potato and return it to the pan. Peel the garlic and add it to the potato, then mash together and strain in the saffron milk. Keep mashing until smooth, then stir in the fish, flour, 1 teaspoon of the lemon zest, the parsley and cream. Season. Shape the mixture into eight even-sized cakes and refrigerate.

Make the herbed crème fraîche by mixing together the crème fraîche, remaining lemon zest and herbs. Heat the butter in a large non-stick frying pan and cook the fish cakes for 3 minutes on each side. Serve with the herbed crème fraîche.

SERVES 4

Tuna steaks with olive mayonnaise and wedges

3 large roasting potatoes, unpeeled and
   cut lengthways into 8 wedges
350 ml (12 fl oz) olive oil
2 egg yolks, at room temperature
1 tablespoon lemon juice
4 tablespoons pitted black olives, finely chopped
200 g (7 oz) baby rocket (arugula) leaves
1 tablespoon finely chopped rosemary
4 x 200 g (7 oz) tuna steaks

Preheat the oven to 200°C (400°F/Gas 6). Toss the potatoes with 2 tablespoons oil in a roasting tin. Bake for 45–50 minutes, or until crisp and golden.

Meanwhile, process the egg yolks in a food processor, adding 3 tablespoons of the oil drop by drop. With the motor running, pour in 185 ml (6 fl oz/¾ cup) of the oil in a thin stream until the mixture thickens and becomes creamy. With the motor still running, add 1 teaspoon of the lemon juice, season with salt and blend for 30 seconds. Stir in the olives, cover and refrigerate.

To make the salad, toss the rocket leaves, 2 tablespoons oil and remaining lemon juice in a bowl.

Press the rosemary into the tuna steaks. Heat the remaining tablespoon of oil in a large frying pan and sear the tuna steaks over medium–high heat for 2–3 minutes on each side, or until cooked to your liking. Serve with a dollop of olive mayonnaise, some potato wedges and rocket salad.

SERVES 4

Blackened snapper

6 large skinless snapper fillets, 2 cm (¾ inch) thick
125 g (4½ oz) unsalted butter, melted
2 tablespoons Cajun spice mix
2 teaspoons sweet paprika
lemon slices, to serve

Brush each fish fillet liberally with the melted butter.

Combine the Cajun spice mix and paprika, then sprinkle thickly over the fish.
Use your fingers to rub the spice mix evenly over the fillets.

Heat a large frying pan over high heat. Cook two fillets at a time in the pan for
1–2 minutes on one side. Turn and cook for another few minutes, or until the fish
is cooked and flakes easily. The surface should be well charred on each side. Add
extra butter if necessary. Serve drizzled with any remaining melted butter and
lemon wedges — they can be served lightly charred if you like.

SERVES 6

Fish Provençale

1 small red capsicum (pepper), thinly sliced
250 g (9 oz/1 cup) tomato pasta sauce
1 tablespoon chopped thyme
40 g (1½ oz) butter
4 x 200 g (7 oz) skinless perch or snapper fillets
thyme sprigs, to garnish

Put the capsicum, pasta sauce and chopped thyme in a bowl and mix well.

Melt half the butter in a large non-stick frying pan over high heat and cook the fish for 1 minute, adding the remaining butter as you go. Turn the fish over and pour on the capsicum mixture. Simmer for 10 minutes, or until the fish is cooked. Season to taste and garnish with thyme sprigs. Serve with roasted potato slices and crusty bread to soak up the juices.

SERVES 4

Singapore pepper crab

2 tablespoons dark soy sauce

2 tablespoons oyster sauce

1 tablespoon grated palm sugar (jaggery) or soft brown sugar

2 kg (4 lb 8 oz) blue swimmer crabs

1–2 tablespoons oil

150 g (5½ oz) butter

2 tablespoons finely chopped garlic

1 tablespoon finely chopped fresh ginger

1 small red chilli, seeded and finely chopped

1½ tablespoons ground black pepper

1 spring onion (scallion), green part only, thinly sliced on the diagonal

To make the stir-fry sauce, mix the soy sauce, oyster sauce and sugar in a small bowl and set aside.

Wash the crabs well with a stiff brush. Pull back the apron and remove the top shell from each crab (it should come off easily). Remove the intestine and the grey feathery gills. Using a large sharp knife, cut the crab lengthways through the centre of the body to form two halves with the legs attached. Cut each half in half again, crossways. Crack the thicker part of the legs with the back of a heavy knife or crab crackers.

Heat a wok over high heat, add a little oil and swirl to coat. Add the crab in a few batches, stir-frying over very high heat for 4 minutes each batch, or until the shells turn bright orange, adding more oil if needed. Remove from the wok. Reduce the heat to medium–high, add the butter, garlic, ginger, chilli and pepper and stir-fry for 30 seconds, then add the stir-fry sauce and simmer for 1 minute, or until glossy.

Return the crab to the wok, cover and stir every minute for 4 minutes, or until cooked. Sprinkle with the spring onion and serve with rice. Provide bowls of warm water with lemon slices for rinsing sticky fingers.

SERVES 4

Lemon and pepper tuna burger

2 x 185 g (6½ oz) tins lemon
    pepper tuna, drained
1 large onion, chopped
65 g (2½ oz/⅔ cup) dry
    breadcrumbs
1 egg, lightly beaten
2 tablespoons chopped lemon
    thyme
1 tablespoon chopped flat-leaf
    (Italian) parsley

2 teaspoons grated lemon zest
2 tablespoons olive oil
1 loaf pide (Turkish/flat) bread
4 tablespoons whole-egg
    mayonnaise
150 g (5½ oz) rocket (arugula)
4 slices cheddar cheese
2 tomatoes, sliced
1 cucumber, sliced
½ red onion, sliced

Mix the tuna, onion, breadcrumbs, egg, thyme, parsley and lemon zest in a bowl. Form into four even-sized patties and flatten slightly. Heat a non-stick frying pan with the oil. Cook the patties over medium heat on both sides for 5 minutes, or until browned.

Cut the bread into four portions. Cut each portion in half horizontally and place under a grill (broiler) to lightly brown.

Spread both cut sides of the bread with mayonnaise. Top with some rocket and layer with a patty, a slice of cheese and slices of tomato, cucumber and onion. Place the other half of the bread on top, cut in half and serve.

SERVES 4

Sweet citrus scallop salad

Lemon and herb dressing
½ preserved lemon
3 tablespoons olive oil
2 tablespoons lemon juice
1 tablespoon sweet chilli sauce
2 tablespoons white wine vinegar
2 tablespoons chopped coriander (cilantro) leaves

500 g (1 lb 2 oz) all-purpose potatoes
olive oil, for shallow-frying
2 tablespoons olive oil, extra
750 g (1 lb 10 oz) scallops, without roe,
   membrane removed
80 g (2¾ oz) baby English spinach leaves

For the dressing, scoop out and discard the pulp from the preserved lemon, wash the skin and cut into thin slices. Put in a bowl and whisk with the olive oil, lemon juice, sweet chilli sauce, vinegar and coriander.

Cut the potatoes into paper-thin slices. Heat 2 cm (¾ inch) oil in a deep heavy-based frying pan and cook batches of the potato for 1–2 minutes, or until crisp and golden. Drain on crumpled paper towels.

Heat the extra oil in a frying pan over high heat and cook the scallops in batches for 1–2 minutes, or until they are golden brown on both sides.

Divide half the spinach among four plates. Top with potato, then half the scallops and more spinach. Finish with more scallops. Drizzle with the lemon and herb dressing just before serving.

SERVES 4

Prawn tacos

2 firm ripe tomatoes, seeded and diced
2 tablespoons lime juice
½ teaspoon chilli powder
½ teaspoon ground cumin
2 tablespoons oil
1 red onion, diced
4 garlic cloves, crushed
18 raw medium prawns (shrimp), peeled,
   deveined and roughly chopped
3 tablespoons chopped flat-leaf (Italian) parsley
8 taco shells
150 g (5½ oz) iceberg lettuce, shredded
1 avocado, diced
125 g (4½ oz/½ cup) sour cream

Preheat the oven to 180°C (350°F/ Gas 4). Combine the tomato, lime juice, chilli powder and cumin.

Heat the oil in a frying pan, add the onion and garlic and cook gently for 3–5 minutes, or until soft. Add the prawns and toss briefly, then stir in the tomato mixture and cook for another 3–5 minutes, or until the prawns are pink and cooked. Stir in the parsley. Meanwhile, heat the taco shells on a baking tray in the oven for 5 minutes.

Place some lettuce in the bottom of each taco shell, then fill with the prawn mixture. Top with some avocado and a dollop of sour cream.

SERVES 4

Basic pan-fried fish

2–3 tablespoons plain (all-purpose) flour
4 firm white fish cutlets
olive oil, for shallow-frying

Sift the flour together with a little salt and freshly ground black pepper onto a plate. Pat the fish dry with paper towels, then coat both sides of the cutlets with seasoned flour, shaking off any excess.

Heat about 3 mm (⅛ inch) oil in a large frying pan until very hot. Put the fish into the hot oil and cook for 3 minutes on one side, then turn and cook the other side for 2 minutes, or until the coating is crisp and well browned. Reduce the heat to low and cook for another 2–3 minutes, or until the flesh flakes easily when tested with a fork.

Remove the fish from the pan and drain briefly on crumpled paper towels. If you are cooking in batches, keep warm while cooking the remaining cutlets. Serve immediately with a salad or steamed vegetables.

SERVES 4

Sweet chilli prawns

1 kg (2 lb 4 oz) raw medium
   prawns (shrimp)
2 tablespoons oil
1 x 3 cm (½ x 1¼ inch) piece
   fresh ginger, cut into
   matchsticks
2 garlic cloves, finely chopped
5 spring onions (scallions), cut
   into 3 cm (1¼ inch) lengths
4 tablespoons chilli garlic sauce
2 tablespoons tomato sauce

2 tablespoons Chinese rice wine
1 tablespoon Chinese black
   vinegar or rice vinegar (see
   Note)
1 tablespoon soy sauce
1 tablespoon soft brown sugar
1 teaspoon cornflour
   (cornstarch) mixed with
   125 ml (4 fl oz/½ cup) water
finely chopped spring onion
   (scallion), to garnish

Peel and devein the prawns, leaving the tails intact. Heat a wok until very hot, then add the oil and swirl to coat the side. Heat over high heat until smoking, then quickly add the ginger, garlic and spring onion and stir-fry for 1 minute. Add the prawns and cook for 2 minutes, or until they are just pink and starting to curl. Remove the prawns from the wok with tongs or a slotted spoon.

Put the chilli garlic sauce, tomato sauce, rice wine, vinegar, soy sauce, sugar and cornflour paste in a small bowl and whisk together. Pour the sauce into the wok and cook, stirring, for 1–2 minutes, or until it thickens slightly. Return the prawns to the wok for 1–2 minutes, or until heated and cooked through. Garnish with the finely chopped spring onion. Serve immediately with rice or thin egg noodles.

SERVES 4

NOTE: Chinese black vinegar is made from rice and has a sweet, mild taste. It is available in Asian food stores.

Tuna and green bean stir-fry

300 g (10½ oz) small green beans, trimmed
2 tablespoons oil
600 g (1 lb 5 oz) piece of tuna, cut into bite-sized cubes
250 g (9 oz) small cherry tomatoes
16 small black olives
2–3 tablespoons lemon juice
2 garlic cloves, finely chopped
8 anchovy fillets, rinsed, dried and finely chopped
3 tablespoons small basil leaves

Blanch the beans in a small saucepan of boiling water for 2 minutes. Drain and refresh under cold water, then set aside.

Heat a wok until very hot, add the oil and swirl to coat the side. Stir-fry the tuna in batches for about 5 minutes each batch, or until cooked on the outside but still a little pink on the inside.

Add the cherry tomatoes, olives and beans to the wok, then gently toss until heated through. Add the lemon juice, garlic and anchovies and stir well. Season to taste with salt and freshly ground black pepper. Serve scattered with the basil leaves.

SERVES 4

Stir-fried scallops with sugar snap peas

2 tablespoons oil
2 large garlic cloves, crushed
3 teaspoons finely chopped fresh ginger
300 g (10½ oz) sugar snap peas
500 g (1 lb 2 oz) scallops, without roe,
    membrane removed
2 spring onions (scallions), cut into
    2 cm (¾ inch) lengths
2½ tablespoons oyster sauce
2 teaspoons soy sauce
½ teaspoon sesame oil
2 teaspoons sugar

Heat a wok over medium heat, add the oil and swirl to coat the side. Add the garlic and ginger, and stir-fry for 30 seconds, or until fragrant.

Add the peas to the wok and cook for 1 minute, then add the scallops and spring onion and cook for 1 minute, or until the spring onion is wilted. Stir in the oyster and soy sauces, sesame oil and sugar and heat for 1 minute, or until warmed through. Serve with rice.

SERVES 4

Prawn and snow pea stir-fry

1½ tablespoons oil
3 garlic cloves, thinly sliced
1 lemongrass stem, white part only, finely chopped
1½ tablespoons thinly sliced fresh ginger
1 kg (2 lb 4 oz) raw medium prawns (shrimp),
    peeled and deveined, tails intact
200 g (7 oz) snow peas (mangetout), trimmed and
    cut into 3–4 strips lengthways
6 spring onions (scallions), thinly sliced on the diagonal
80 g (2¾ oz) snow pea (mangetout) sprouts
1 tablespoon Chinese rice wine
1 tablespoon oyster sauce
1 tablespoon soy sauce

Heat a wok to very hot, add the oil and swirl to coat the side. Add the garlic, lemongrass and ginger and stir-fry for 1–2 minutes, or until fragrant. Add the prawns and cook for 2–3 minutes, or until pink and cooked.

Add the snow peas, spring onion, sprouts, rice wine, oyster and soy sauces and toss until heated through and the vegetables start to wilt.

SERVES 4–6

Salmon and dill potato patties with lime mayonnaise

400 g (14 oz) new potatoes, halved
2 teaspoons grated lime zest
310 g (11 oz/1¼ cups) whole-egg mayonnaise
425 g (15 oz) tin salmon, drained, bones removed
1 tablespoon chopped dill
2 spring onions (scallions), thinly sliced
1 egg, lightly beaten
80 g (2¾ oz/1 cup) fresh breadcrumbs
3 tablespoons olive oil
200 g (7 oz) rocket (arugula) leaves
lime wedges, to serve

Cook the potatoes in a large saucepan of boiling water for 12–15 minutes, or until tender. Drain well and cool.

Meanwhile, combine the lime zest and 250 g (9 oz/1 cup) of the mayonnaise.

Transfer the potato to a large bowl, then mash roughly with the back of a spoon, leaving some large chunks. Stir in the salmon, dill and spring onion and season. Mix in the egg and the remaining mayonnaise. Divide into eight portions, forming palm-size patties. Press lightly into the breadcrumbs to coat.

Heat the oil in a non-stick frying pan and cook the patties for 3–4 minutes, or until golden brown on both sides. Drain on crumpled paper towels. Serve with a dollop of lime mayonnaise, some rocket leaves and lime wedges.

SERVES 4

Beer-battered fish
with crunchy fries

155 g (5½ oz/1¼ cups) plain (all-purpose) flour
375 ml (13 fl oz/1½ cups) beer
4 roasting potatoes, cut into 1 cm (½ inch) wide strips
oil, for deep-frying
4 x 200 g (7 oz) skinless firm white fish fillets, patted dry
cornflour (cornstarch), for coating
lemon wedges, to serve

Sift the flour into a large bowl and make a well in the centre. Gradually pour in the beer, whisking to make a smooth batter. Cover and set aside.

Soak the potatoes in cold water for 10 minutes. Drain and pat dry. Fill a wok or deep-fat fryer one-third full of oil and heat to 160°C (320°F), or until a small cube of bread browns in 30 seconds. Cook batches of the potato for 4–5 minutes, or until golden. Remove with a slotted spoon and drain on crumpled paper towels.

Dust the fish with cornflour, dip into the batter and shake off any excess. Deep-fry in batches for 5–7 minutes, or until golden and the fish is cooked through. Turn with tongs if necessary. You can check that the fish is cooked by cutting into the centre of one of the pieces — the flesh should be moist and opaque. Drain on crumpled paper towels. Keep warm in a low oven while you cook the fries again. Reheat the oil to 180°C (350°F), or until a cube of white bread browns in 15 seconds. Cook the fries for 1–2 minutes, in batches, until crisp and golden. Drain on crumpled paper towels. Serve the fish with lemon wedges and the fries.

SERVES 4

Mahi mahi with lime sauce

4 x 200 g (7 oz) skinless mahi mahi fillets
zest and juice of 2 limes
100 ml (3½ fl oz) dry white wine
1 large garlic clove, cut into slivers
200 g (7 oz) unsalted butter, chilled
2 tablespoons olive oil

Put the fish fillets in a non-metallic dish. Mix the lime zest and juice, wine and garlic together and pour over the fish. Turn the fish and leave to marinate for 30 minutes, turning now and then. Meanwhile, cut the butter into cubes and return to the fridge.

Transfer the fish to a plate. Strain the marinade through a sieve into a small saucepan. Bring the marinade to the boil and simmer until reduced to 2 tablespoons.

Meanwhile, heat the oil in a large frying pan. When hot, add half of the fish and cook for 3–4 minutes, turning once, or until opaque and cooked through. Repeat with the rest of the fish and keep warm in a low oven.

Over a low heat, whisk the butter, cube by cube, into the liquid left in the saucepan, whisking thoroughly after each addition. When half of the butter has been incorporated, a few cubes can be added at a time. Do not allow the sauce to overheat. When all the butter has been incorporated, season to taste. Serve the sauce with the fish, along with some steamed green beans.

SERVES 4

Salmon in nori with noodles

4 salmon cutlets, cut from the
    centre of the fish
    (ask your fishmonger)
1 sheet of nori (dried seaweed)
2 teaspoons oil
250 g (9 oz) somen noodles
2 spring onions (scallions), cut
    into long thin strips

Dressing
½–¾ teaspoon wasabi paste
2 tablespoons rice vinegar
2 tablespoons mirin
1 tablespoon lime juice
2 teaspoons soft brown sugar
1 tablespoon oil
2 teaspoons soy sauce
2 teaspoons black sesame seeds,
    plus some extra, to garnish

Remove the skin and bones from the salmon, keeping the cutlets in one piece. Cut the nori into strips, the same width as the salmon, and wrap a strip tightly around each cutlet to form a neat circle. Seal the edges with a little water. Season with salt and freshly ground black pepper.

Heat the oil in a frying pan and cook the salmon for 2–3 minutes on each side, or until cooked to your liking (ideally, it should be a little pink in the centre).

While the salmon is cooking, prepare the noodles and dressing. Put the noodles in a large bowl, cover with boiling water and stand for 5 minutes, or until softened. Drain well. Combine the dressing ingredients in a small bowl and mix well.

Divide the noodles among serving plates, top with a salmon cutlet and drizzle with the dressing. Add the spring onion, then sprinkle with sesame seeds.

SERVES 4

Stir-fried squid flowers with capsicum

400 g (14 oz) squid tubes
3 tablespoons oil
2 tablespoons salted, fermented black beans,
    rinsed and drained, then mashed (see Note)
1 small onion, diced
1 small green capsicum (pepper), diced
3–4 small fresh ginger slices
1 spring onion (scallion), cut into short lengths
1 small red chilli, chopped
1 tablespoon Chinese rice wine
½ teaspoon sesame oil

Open up the squid tube and scrub off any soft jelly-like substance, then score the inside of the flesh with a fine crisscross pattern, making sure you do not cut all the way through. Cut the squid into pieces that are about 3 x 5 cm (1¼ x 2 inches).

Blanch the squid in a saucepan of boiling water for 25–30 seconds — each piece will curl up and the crisscross pattern will open out, hence the name 'squid flower'. Remove and refresh in cold water, then drain and dry well.

Heat a wok over high heat, add the oil and swirl to coat the side. Stir-fry the black beans, onion, capsicum, ginger, spring onion and chilli for 1 minute. Add the squid and rice wine, blend well and stir for 1 minute. Sprinkle with the sesame oil.

SERVES 4 AS A STARTER

NOTE: Salted fermented black beans are fermented soya beans that have a distinct, salty flavour. They can be bought from Asian food stores.

Fish fillets with fennel and red capsicum salsa

750 g (1 lb 10 oz) small new
  potatoes
1 teaspoon fennel seeds
125 ml (4 fl oz/½ cup) olive oil
2 tablespoons baby capers,
  rinsed and squeezed dry
1 small red capsicum (pepper),
  seeded and finely diced

250 g (9 oz) mixed salad leaves,
  washed and picked over
2 tablespoons balsamic vinegar
4 x 200 g (7 oz) skinless firm
  white fish fillets, such as blue
  eye or john dory

Cook the potatoes in a saucepan of boiling water for 15–20 minutes, or until tender. Drain and keep warm.

Meanwhile, to make the salsa, dry-fry the fennel seeds in a frying pan over medium heat for 1 minute, or until fragrant. Remove the seeds and heat 1 tablespoon oil in the same pan over medium heat. When the oil is hot but not smoking, flash-fry the capers for 1–2 minutes, or until crisp. Remove from the pan. Heat 1 tablespoon oil and cook the capsicum, stirring, for 4–5 minutes, or until cooked through. Remove and combine with the fennel seeds and fried capers.

Place the salad leaves in a serving bowl. To make the dressing, combine the balsamic vinegar and 3 tablespoons of the olive oil in a bowl. Add 1 tablespoon to the salsa, then toss the rest through the salad leaves.

Wipe the frying pan, then heat the remaining oil over medium–high heat. Season the fish well. When the oil is hot, but not smoking, cook the fish for 2–3 minutes each side, or until cooked through. Serve immediately with the salsa, potatoes and salad.

SERVES 4

Lemon and thyme tuna with tagliatelle

375 g (13 oz) tagliatelle
145 ml (4¾ fl oz) extra virgin olive oil
1 small red chilli, seeded and finely chopped
3 tablespoons drained capers
1½ tablespoons lemon thyme leaf tips
500 g (1 lb 2 oz) tuna steaks, trimmed and
   cut into 3 cm (1¼ inch) cubes
3 tablespoons lemon juice
1 tablespoon grated lemon zest
3 large handfuls flat-leaf (Italian) parsley, chopped

Cook the tagliatelle in a large saucepan of rapidly boiling salted water until *al dente*. Drain, then return to the pan.

Meanwhile, heat 1 tablespoon of the oil in a large frying pan. Add the chilli and capers and cook, stirring, for 1 minute, or until the capers are crisp. Add the thyme and cook for another minute. Transfer to a bowl.

Heat another tablespoon of oil in the pan. Add the tuna cubes and toss for 2–3 minutes, or until evenly browned on the outside but still pink in the centre — check with the point of a sharp knife. Remove from the heat.

Add the tuna to the caper mixture along with the lemon juice, lemon zest, parsley and the remaining oil, stirring gently until combined. Toss through the pasta, season with freshly ground black pepper and serve immediately.

SERVES 4

Scallops in black bean sauce

2 tablespoons oil
24 scallops, without roe, membrane removed
1 tablespoon soy sauce
2 tablespoons Chinese rice wine
1 teaspoon sugar
1 garlic clove, finely chopped
1 spring onion (scallion), finely chopped
½ teaspoon finely grated fresh ginger
1 tablespoon salted, fermented black beans,
   rinsed and drained (see Note)
1 teaspoon sesame oil

Heat 1 tablespoon of the oil in a wok and swirl to coat the side. Add the scallops and cook for 2 minutes, or until firm. Remove to a plate.

Mix together the soy sauce, rice wine and sugar in a cup with a tablespoon of water and set aside.

Add the remaining oil to the wok and heat until it is beginning to smoke. Add the garlic, spring onion and ginger. Cook for 30 seconds. Add the beans and the soy sauce mixture and bring to the boil. Return the scallops to the sauce with the sesame oil and allow to simmer for about 30 seconds. Serve immediately with rice and steamed Asian greens.

SERVES 4

NOTE: Salted fermented black beans are fermented soya beans that have a distinct, salty flavour. They are used in the cooking of southern China. You can buy them from Asian food stores and some supermarkets.

Sesame-coated tuna with coriander salsa

4 tuna steaks
115 g (4 oz/¾ cup) sesame seeds
100 g (3½ oz) baby rocket (arugula) leaves

Coriander salsa
2 tomatoes, seeded and diced
1 large garlic clove, crushed
2 tablespoons finely chopped coriander (cilantro) leaves
2 tablespoons virgin olive oil, plus extra for shallow-frying
1 tablespoon lime juice

Cut each tuna steak into three pieces. Place the sesame seeds on a sheet of baking paper. Roll the tuna in the sesame seeds to coat. Refrigerate for 15 minutes.

To make the salsa, place the tomato, garlic, coriander, oil and lime juice in a bowl and mix together well. Cover and refrigerate until ready to use.

Fill a heavy-based frying pan to 1.5 cm (⅝ inch) with the extra oil and place over high heat. Add the tuna in two batches and cook for 2 minutes each side (it should be pink in the centre). Remove and drain on crumpled paper towels. To serve, divide the rocket among four serving plates and arrange the tuna over the top. Spoon the salsa on the side and serve immediately. Top with a teaspoon of chilli jam, if desired, and season.

SERVES 4

Sole meunière

4 Dover sole, gutted and dark skin removed
3 tablespoons plain (all-purpose) flour
200 g (7 oz) clarified butter (see Note)
2 tablespoons lemon juice
4 tablespoons chopped flat-leaf (Italian) parsley
lemon wedges, to serve

Pat the fish dry with paper towels, cut the fine bones and frill of skin away from around the edge of the fish, remove the heads if you prefer, and then dust lightly with the flour and season. Heat 150 g (5½ oz) of the butter in a frying pan large enough to fit all four fish, or use half the butter and cook the fish in two batches.

Put the fish in the pan, skin-side up, and cook for 4 minutes, or until golden (this will be the service side), turn over carefully and cook on the other side for another 4 minutes, or until the fish is cooked through (the flesh will feel firm). Lift the fish out onto warm plates and drizzle with the lemon juice and sprinkle with the parsley. Add the remaining butter to the pan and heat until it browns, but be careful not to overbrown it or the sauce will taste burnt. Pour over the fish (it will foam as it mixes with the lemon juice) and serve with lemon wedges and steamed greens.

SERVES 4

NOTE: Clarified butter has a higher burning point than other butters. To clarify butter, heat a pack of butter until liquid. Leave until the white milk solids settle to the bottom of the saucepan. Use a spoon to skim off any foam, then strain off the golden liquid, discarding the white solids that are left behind.

oven

Tandoori prawn pizza

1 tablespoon olive oil

2 teaspoons paprika

½ teaspoon ground cumin

¼ teaspoon ground cardamom

¼ teaspoon ground ginger

¼ teaspoon cayenne pepper

4 tablespoons Greek-style yoghurt,
   plus extra, to serve

1 teaspoon lemon juice

2 garlic cloves, crushed

16 raw medium prawns (shrimp),
   peeled and deveined, tails intact

30 cm (12 inch) ready-made pizza base

1 onion, sliced

1 small red capsicum (pepper), sliced

3 tablespoons torn basil

Preheat the oven to 220°C (425°F/Gas 7). To make the tandoori sauce, heat the oil in a frying pan over medium heat, add the spices and cook until the oil starts to bubble, then cook for another minute. Stir in the yoghurt, lemon juice and garlic, then add the prawns. Cook for 5 minutes, or until the prawns are pink and cooked.

Remove the prawns from the tandoori sauce with a slotted spoon and spread the sauce over the pizza base, leaving a 1 cm (½ inch) border. Sprinkle with some of the onion and capsicum, then arrange the prawns on top. Top with the remaining onion and capsicum and bake for about 20 minutes. Scatter with the basil, then serve with the extra yoghurt.

SERVES 4

Idaho trout parcels

25 g (1 oz) butter
1 tablespoon olive oil, plus a little for the parcels
1 French shallot, finely chopped
225 g (8 oz) small mushrooms, sliced
2 tablespoons tarragon vinegar
1 tablespoon chopped tarragon
4 x 175–225 g (6–8 oz) pieces of skinless trout

Preheat the oven to 220°C (425°F/Gas 7). Heat the butter and oil in a frying pan, then cook the shallot for 2–3 minutes, or until softened. Add the mushrooms and stir to coat them in the oil and butter. Cook for 5 minutes, stirring every now and then. Splash in the vinegar and bubble away for 30 seconds. Take the pan off the heat and stir in the tarragon. Season with salt and freshly ground black pepper.

Lightly oil four 35 cm (14 inch) rounds of heavy-duty baking paper. Fold in half to make a crease in the middle and then unfold again. Lay them oil-side up. Put a piece of fish on one half of each circle. Top with the mushroom mixture, dividing it equally among the fish. Fold the empty half of the circle over the fish and fold the edges of the circle twice and pinch together to seal firmly. Do the same for each one. Lay the parcels on a large baking tray and bake for 10–15 minutes. Transfer the parcels to serving plates and let everyone open their own.

SERVES 4

Baked swordfish steaks with salsa verde

4 x 200 g (7 oz) swordfish steaks

Salsa verde
2 tablespoons olive oil
1 large onion, finely chopped
1 garlic clove, finely chopped
1 large green capsicum (pepper)
40 g (1½ oz) jalapeño chillies
2 tablespoons roughly chopped
   coriander (cilantro) leaves

Preheat the oven to 180°C (350°F/Gas 4). Put the swordfish steaks in a large rectangular ovenproof dish.

To make the salsa verde, heat 1 tablespoon of the oil in a small saucepan and, when hot, add the onion and garlic and cook for 10 minutes, or until the onion has softened. Allow to cool for a few minutes. Blanch the capsicum in boiling water for 8 minutes, then drain. Put the softened onion and garlic in a food processor with the capsicum, chillies, coriander and remaining oil. Blend to a purée and season with salt. Alternatively, finely chop the ingredients by hand and mix together well.

Spread the salsa verde on top of the swordfish steaks, dividing it equally. Bake in the preheated oven for 20–25 minutes, or until the fish is firm and opaque. Serve with crispy baked potato chunks.

SERVES 4

Fish pie

Potato topping

500 g (1 lb 2 oz) all-purpose
    potatoes, diced
3 tablespoons milk
1 egg, lightly beaten
30 g (1 oz) butter
60 g (2¼ oz) cheddar cheese,
    finely grated

800 g (1 lb 12 oz) skinless firm
    white fish fillets, cut into
    large chunks

375 ml (13 fl oz/1½ cups) milk
30 g (1 oz) butter
1 onion, finely chopped
1 garlic clove, crushed
2 tablespoons plain
    (all-purpose) flour
2 tablespoons lemon juice
2 teaspoons lemon zest
1 tablespoon chopped dill

Preheat the oven to 180°C (350°F/Gas 4). To make the topping, steam the potato until tender. Mash, then push to one side of the pan, add the milk and heat gently. Beat the milk into the potato until it is fluffy, then season and stir in the egg and butter. Mix in half the cheddar, then set aside and keep warm.

Put the fish in a frying pan and cover with the milk. Bring to the boil, then reduce the heat and simmer for 2 minutes, or until the fish is opaque and flaky. Drain, reserving the milk, and put the fish in a 1.5 litre (52 fl oz/6 cup) ovenproof dish.

Melt the butter in a saucepan and cook the onion and garlic for 2 minutes. Stir in the flour and cook for 1 minute, or until pale and foaming. Remove from the heat and gradually stir in the reserved milk. Return to the heat and stir constantly until it boils and thickens. Reduce the heat and simmer for 2 minutes. Add the lemon juice, zest and dill, and season. Mix with the fish. Spoon the topping over the fish and top with the remaining cheddar. Bake for 35 minutes, or until golden.

SERVES 4

Jansson's temptation

15 anchovy fillets
4 tablespoons milk
60 g (2¼ oz) butter
2 large onions, thinly sliced
5 all-purpose potatoes, cut into 5 mm (¼ inch)
    thick slices, then cut into matchsticks
500 g (1 lb 2 oz/2¼ cups) thick
    (double/heavy) cream

Preheat the oven to 200°C (400°F/Gas 6). Soak the anchovies in the milk for
5 minutes to lessen their saltiness. Drain and rinse.

Melt half the butter in a frying pan and cook the onion over medium heat for
5 minutes, or until golden and tender. Chop the remaining butter into small cubes
and set aside.

Spread half the potato over the base of a shallow ovenproof dish, top with the
anchovies and onion and finish with the remaining potato.

Pour half the cream over the potato and scatter the butter cubes on top. Bake for
20 minutes, or until golden. Pour the remaining cream over the top and cook for
another 40 minutes, or until the potato feels tender when the point of a knife is
inserted. Season with salt and pepper before serving.

SERVES 4

Aromatic snapper parcels

3 handfuls basil, chopped
2 large garlic cloves, chopped
1 tablespoon lemon juice
1 teaspoon grated lemon zest
3 tablespoons olive oil
4 x 200 g (7 oz) skinless snapper
 fillets, trimmed and boned

500 g (1 lb 2 oz) small new
 potatoes
20 asparagus spears, trimmed
12 yellow baby (pattypan)
 squash

Preheat the oven to 200°C (400°F/Gas 6). Combine the basil, garlic, lemon juice, zest and 2 tablespoons of the olive oil. Season.

Place a fish fillet in the centre of a sheet of foil large enough to fully enclose it. Season with salt and pepper. Smear the fillet with 2 teaspoons of the basil mixture, then wrap into a secure parcel with the foil. Repeat with the remaining fillets. Place on a baking tray and refrigerate until required.

Cook the potatoes in a saucepan of boiling water for 15–20 minutes, or until tender. Drain and keep warm. While the potatoes are cooking, brush the asparagus and squash with the remaining oil. Place on a baking tray and season with freshly ground black pepper. Bake for 8–10 minutes, or until golden and tender.

About 10 minutes before the vegetables are ready, place the fish parcels in the oven and cook for 5–7 minutes, or until the flesh flakes easily when tested with a fork. Check one of the parcels after 5 minutes to see if the fish is cooked through. Place the opened parcels on serving plates with the vegetables, season to taste and serve.

SERVES 4

Blue eye cutlets in a spicy tomato sauce

4 blue eye cutlets, 2.5 cm (1 inch) thick (about 250 g/9 oz each)
250 g (9 oz/1¼ cups) long-grain rice
2 tablespoons oil
1 teaspoon coriander seeds, lightly crushed
1 teaspoon black mustard seeds
1½ tablespoons sambal oelek
400 g (14 oz) tin diced tomatoes
1 teaspoon garam masala
300 g (10½ oz) baby English spinach leaves

Preheat the oven to 180°C (350°F/Gas 4). Pat the cutlets dry with paper towels. Bring a large saucepan of water to the boil. Add the rice and cook for 12 minutes, stirring occasionally. Drain well.

Meanwhile, heat 1 tablespoon of the oil in a saucepan over medium heat. When hot, add the coriander and mustard seeds — the mustard seeds should start to pop after 30 seconds. Add the sambal oelek and cook for 30 seconds, then stir in the tomatoes and garam masala. Bring to the boil, then reduce the heat to low and simmer, covered, for 6–8 minutes, or until the sauce thickens.

Heat the remaining oil in a large non-stick frying pan over medium heat. Add the cutlets and cook for 1 minute each side, or until evenly browned but not cooked through. Transfer to a 18.5 x 28 cm (7 x 11¼ inch) ceramic baking dish. Spoon the tomato sauce over the cutlets and bake for 10 minutes, or until the fish is cooked through.

Meanwhile, wash the spinach and put in a saucepan with just the water clinging to the leaves. Cook, covered, for 1 minute, or until wilted. Serve the fish cutlets on a bed of rice, topped with sauce, and the spinach alongside.

SERVES 4

Tuna bake

200 g (7 oz) short curly pasta
  such as cotelli or fusilli
4 eggs, hard-boiled and roughly
  chopped
4 spring onions (scallions), finely
  chopped
1 tablespoon chopped dill
1 tablespoon lemon juice
115 g (4 oz) butter
3 teaspoons madras curry
  powder
4 tablespoons plain
  (all-purpose) flour
375 ml (13 fl oz/1½ cups) milk

375 ml (13 fl oz/1½ cups)
  pouring (whipping) cream
175 g (6 oz) whole-egg
  mayonnaise
3 x 210 g (7½ oz) tins tuna,
  drained
160 g (5¾ oz/2 cups) fresh white
  breadcrumbs
1 garlic clove, crushed
1 tablespoon finely chopped
  flat-leaf (Italian) parsley
2 tablespoons grated parmesan
  cheese

Preheat the oven to 180°C (350°F/Gas 4). Cook the pasta in a large saucepan of boiling salted water until *al dente*. Drain. Lightly grease a 2 litre (70 fl oz/8 cup) ovenproof dish. Combine the egg, spring onion, dill and lemon juice and season.

Melt 60 g (2¼ oz) of the butter in a saucepan, add the curry powder and cook for 30 seconds. Stir in the flour and cook until foaming. Remove from the heat, gradually stir in the milk and cream, then return to low heat and stir constantly until the sauce boils and thickens. Simmer for 2 minutes, then stir in the mayonnaise. Combine the sauce, pasta, tuna and egg mixture and spoon into your dish.

Melt the remaining butter in a frying pan, add the breadcrumbs and garlic and cook, stirring, for 1 minute, or until the breadcrumbs are golden. Stir in the parsley and parmesan, then sprinkle over the tuna mixture. Bake for 15–20 minutes.

SERVES 6

Mexican baked fish

3 firm, ripe tomatoes, chopped
½ teaspoon ground cumin
½ teaspoon ground allspice
½ teaspoon ground cinnamon
1 habañero chilli, seeded and finely chopped
4 tablespoons coriander (cilantro) leaves
4 x 175–200 g (6–7 oz) skinless red snapper or cod fillets
½ small red onion, chopped
½ small green capsicum (pepper), chopped
1 tablespoon sour or Seville orange juice,
    or 2 teaspoons orange juice and 2 teaspoons vinegar
juice of 1 lime

Preheat the oven to 190°C (375°F/Gas 5). Mix the tomatoes in a bowl with the cumin, allspice, cinnamon, chilli and coriander.

Place a piece of fish in the centre of a sheet of foil large enough to fully enclose it. Top with one-quarter of the tomato mixture, then repeat with the remaining fish and tomato mixture.

Mix the red onion and green capsicum together and divide among the parcels. Combine the orange and lime juice and drizzle over the top of the fish and vegetables. Season with salt and pepper.

Enclose the fish securely in the foil and transfer the parcels to a baking dish. Bake for 15–20 minutes, or until the fish flakes easily when tested with a fork.

SERVES 4

Roast fish with rosemary and garlic

1 kg (2 lb 4 oz) skinless monkfish tail fillets,
   membrane removed, or barramundi fillets
3 large garlic cloves, sliced into thin slivers
1 rosemary stem, cut into 24 small sprigs
6 bacon slices, halved
4 tablespoons olive oil
lemon wedges, to serve

Preheat the oven to 200°C (400°F/Gas 6). Using a small sharp knife, make small incisions in the fish and insert a sliver of garlic and a small sprig of rosemary into each one. Season the fish with salt and pepper and wrap a piece of bacon around each piece of fish.

Put the fish in a roasting tin and drizzle the olive oil over the top. Roast for about 15 minutes, or until the fish is cooked through. Serve with lemon wedges.

SERVES 4

Baked tuna Siciliana

4 tablespoons olive oil

2 tablespoons lemon juice

2½ tablespoons finely chopped basil

4 x 175 g (6 oz) tuna steaks

60 g (2¼ oz) black olives, pitted and chopped

1 tablespoon baby capers, rinsed and patted dry

2 anchovy fillets, finely chopped

400 g (14 oz) tomatoes, peeled, seeded and
   chopped, or a 400 g (14 oz) tin chopped tomatoes

2 tablespoons dry breadcrumbs

Mix 2 tablespoons of the olive oil with the lemon juice and 1 tablespoon of the basil. Season and pour into a shallow, non-metallic ovenproof dish, large enough to hold the tuna steaks in a single layer. Arrange the tuna in the dish and leave to marinate for 15 minutes, turning once. Preheat the oven to 220°C (425°F/Gas 7) and preheat the grill (broiler).

Combine the olives, capers, anchovies and tomatoes with the remaining oil and the remaining basil and season well. Spread over the tuna and sprinkle the breadcrumbs over the top. Bake for about 20 minutes, or until the fish is just opaque. Finish off by placing briefly under the hot grill until the breadcrumbs are crisp. Serve with bread to soak up the juices.

SERVES 4

Thai ginger fish with coriander butter

60 g (2¼ oz) butter, at room temperature
1 tablespoon finely chopped coriander (cilantro) leaves
2 tablespoons lime juice
1 tablespoon oil
1 tablespoon grated palm sugar (jaggery) or soft brown sugar
4 long red chillies, seeded and chopped

2 lemongrass stems, trimmed
4 x 200 g (7 oz) firm white fish fillets, such as blue eye or john dory
1 lime, thinly sliced
1 tablespoon finely shredded fresh ginger

Combine the butter and coriander and roll it into a log. Wrap the log in plastic wrap and refrigerate until required. Preheat the oven to 200°C (400°F/Gas 6).

Combine the lime juice, oil, sugar and chilli in a small non-metallic bowl and stir until the sugar has dissolved. Cut the lemongrass into halves lengthways.

Place a piece of lemongrass in the centre of a sheet of foil large enough to fully enclose one fillet. Place a fish fillet on top and smear the surface with the lime juice mixture. Top with some lime slices and ginger shreds, then wrap into a secure parcel. Repeat with the remaining ingredients to make four parcels.

Place the parcels in an ovenproof dish and bake for 8–10 minutes, or until the fish flakes easily when tested with a fork.

To serve, place the parcels on individual serving plates and serve open with slices of coriander butter, steamed rice and steamed greens.

SERVES 4

Baked Atlantic salmon

16 cherry tomatoes, halved
150 g (5½ oz) fresh, ripe pineapple flesh, diced
4 x 200 g (7 oz) Atlantic salmon fillets, skin on
2 tablespoons balsamic vinegar
2 tablespoons olive oil
100 g (3½ oz) rocket (arugula) or baby English spinach leaves
4 tablespoons shredded basil

Preheat the oven to 180°C (350°F/Gas 4). Mix the tomatoes and pineapple together.

Line a baking tray with a piece of foil, bearing in mind that the foil needs to be large enough to enclose all four salmon fillets. Place the salmon fillets on the foil and season with salt and pepper. Spoon the tomato and pineapple mixture on top of the fillets, dividing it equally. Whisk the balsamic vinegar and olive oil together in a small bowl and drizzle over the top.

Wrap the parcel to enclose the fish and put in the preheated oven for 20–25 minutes, or until the salmon is opaque but still moist and succulent. Open the parcel and spoon on the pineapple and tomato mixture, drizzle with the cooking juices and sprinkle with basil.

Make a small bed of rocket or spinach leaves in the centre of each plate. Lift the salmon fillets out of the foil and sit on top of the leaves.

SERVES 4

Seafood mornay

80 g (2¾ oz) butter
60 g (2¼ oz/½ cup) plain (all-purpose) flour
125 ml (4 fl oz/½ cup) dry white wine
250 ml (9 fl oz/1 cup) thick (double/heavy) cream
250 ml (9 fl oz/1 cup) milk
125 g (4½ oz) cheddar cheese, grated
2 tablespoons wholegrain mustard
1 tablespoon horseradish cream
6 spring onions (scallions), chopped
80 g (2¾ oz/1 cup) fresh breadcrumbs

1 kg (2 lb 4 oz) skinless firm white fish fillets, cut into bite-sized cubes
450 g (1 lb) scallops, without roe, membrane removed
400 g (14 oz) cooked, peeled small prawns (shrimp)

Topping

240 g (8½ oz/3 cups) fresh breadcrumbs
3 tablespoons chopped flat-leaf (Italian) parsley
60 g (2¼ oz) butter, melted
125 g (4½ oz) cheddar cheese, grated

Preheat the oven to 180°C (350°F/Gas 4). Grease a 2 litre (70 fl oz/8 cup) ovenproof dish. Melt 60 g (2¼ oz) of the butter in a saucepan over low heat. Stir in the flour until pale and foaming. Remove from the heat and gradually stir in the wine, cream and milk. Return to high heat and stir until the sauce boils and thickens. Season. Add the cheese, mustard, horseradish, onion and crumbs. Mix well and set aside.

Melt the remaining butter in a large pan and add the fish and scallops in batches. Stir over low heat until the seafood starts to change colour. Drain, add to the sauce along with the prawns, then transfer to your dish. Mix together the topping ingredients and spread over the seafood. Bake for 35 minutes, or until golden.

SERVES 8–10

Prawn pot pies

60 g (2¼ oz) butter
1 leek, white part only, thinly sliced
1 garlic clove, finely chopped
1 kg (2 lb 4 oz) raw medium prawns (shrimp), peeled and deveined
1 tablespoon plain (all-purpose) flour
185 ml (6 fl oz/¾ cup) chicken or fish stock
125 ml (4 fl oz/½ cup) dry white wine

500 ml (17 fl oz/2 cups) pouring (whipping) cream
2 tablespoons lemon juice
1 tablespoon chopped dill
1 tablespoon chopped flat-leaf (Italian) parsley
1 teaspoon dijon mustard
1 sheet frozen puff pastry, just thawed
1 egg, lightly beaten

Preheat the oven to 220°C (425°F/Gas 7). Melt the butter in a saucepan over low heat. Cook the leek and garlic for 2 minutes, then add the prawns and cook for 1–2 minutes. Remove the prawns with a slotted spoon and set aside.

Stir the flour into the pan and cook for 1 minute. Add the stock and wine, bring to the boil and cook for 10 minutes, or until nearly all the liquid has evaporated. Stir in the cream, bring to the boil, then reduce the heat and simmer for 20 minutes, or until the liquid reduces by half. Stir in the lemon juice, herbs and mustard.

Using half the sauce, pour an even amount into four 250 ml (9 fl oz/1 cup) ramekins. Divide the prawns among the ramekins, then top with the remaining sauce.

Cut the pastry into four rounds, slightly larger than the rim of the ramekins. Place the rounds over the filling and press around the edges. Prick the pastry and brush with beaten egg. Bake for 20 minutes, or until golden.

SERVES 4

Greek calamari

Stuffing

1 tablespoon olive oil
280 g (10 oz/1½ cups) cold, cooked rice
60 g (2¼ oz) pine nuts
2 spring onions (scallions), chopped
75 g (2½ oz/½ cup) currants
2 tablespoons chopped flat-leaf (Italian) parsley
2 teaspoons finely grated lemon zest
1 egg, lightly beaten

1 kg (2 lb 4 oz) squid tubes, washed and patted dry

Sauce

4 large ripe tomatoes
1 tablespoon olive oil
1 onion, finely chopped
1 garlic clove, crushed
3 tablespoons good-quality red wine
1 tablespoon chopped oregano

Preheat the oven to 160°C (315°F/Gas 2–3). For the stuffing, mix the oil, rice, pine nuts, spring onion, currants, parsley and lemon zest in a bowl. Season. Add enough egg to moisten the ingredients. Pack each squid tube three-quarters full with the stuffing. Secure the ends with toothpicks. Put in a single layer in a casserole dish.

For the sauce, score a cross in the base of each tomato. Soak in boiling water for 30 seconds, then plunge into cold water. Drain and peel the skin away from the cross. Chop the tomatoes, discarding the cores. Heat the oil in a pan. Add the onion and garlic and cook over low heat for 2 minutes, or until the onion is soft. Add the tomato, wine and oregano and bring to the boil. Reduce the heat, cover and cook over low heat for 10 minutes.

Pour the sauce over the squid, cover and bake for 20 minutes, or until the squid is tender. Remove the toothpicks. Cut into thick slices and spoon over the sauce.

SERVES 4–6

Turbot en papillote with sorrel

25 g (1 oz) butter
1 small onion, finely chopped
125 ml (4 fl oz/½ cup) dry white wine
170 ml (5½ fl oz/⅔ cup) fish stock
2 teaspoons olive oil, for greasing
1.5 kg (3 lb 5 oz) whole turbot, filleted into 4 pieces
2½ tablespoons crème fraîche
3 tablespoons chopped sorrel or basil

Melt the butter in a saucepan and add the onion. Cook for 10 minutes, or until softened but not browned, stirring now and then. Pour in the wine and stock and bring to the boil. Allow to boil for 10–15 minutes, or until reduced by half — you should end up with about 150 ml (5 fl oz).

Preheat the oven to 180°C (350°F/Gas 4). Cut four 30 cm (12 inch) diameter circles from the baking paper. Lightly oil the circles, fold in half to make a crease along the middle and then unfold. Place a piece of fish on one half of each circle.

Once the sauce has reduced, add the crème fraîche. Stir, allow to bubble for 30 seconds, then remove from the heat. Season, stir in the sorrel, and then spoon a quarter of the sauce over the first piece of fish. Fold the empty half of the circle over the fish, fold the edges of the circle over twice and pinch together to seal. Repeat with the other pieces of turbot. As you make the parcels, lift them onto a large baking tray. Bake the fish for 15–20 minutes, depending on the thickness of the fish. Put the parcels on plates so they can be opened at the table.

SERVES 4

Red mullet with baked eggplant

4 x 200 g (7 oz) whole red
   mullet, gutted and scaled

Marinade
pinch saffron threads
125 ml (4 fl oz/½ cup) olive oil
2 tablespoons lemon juice
1 tablespoon pomegranate
   molasses (optional)
1 small onion, grated
1 large garlic clove, crushed
1 tablespoon dried oregano
pinch crushed dried chilli
1 teaspoon nigella seeds

1 teaspoon coriander seeds,
   slightly crushed
1 teaspoon cumin seeds

350 g (12 oz) eggplant
   (aubergine), cut into chunks
80 g (2¾ oz/½ cup) pine nuts,
   lightly toasted
100 g (3½ oz) lamb's lettuce
   (corn salad)
2 tablespoons roughly torn mint
1 tablespoon red wine vinegar
16 small black pitted olives

Lay the fish in a single layer in a shallow non-metallic dish. Infuse the saffron in a tablespoon of hot water for 10 minutes. Mix the saffron and liquid with half of the oil, a pinch of salt and the remaining marinade ingredients. Spread into the central cavity and over the skin of the fish. Cover and marinate in the fridge for 2 hours.

Transfer the fish to a large baking tray and scatter the eggplant around it. Brush both all over with the remaining marinade. Cook under a hot grill (broiler), turning now and then, for 20 minutes, or until the fish and eggplant are cooked through.

Combine the pine nuts, lettuce and mint. Mix the vinegar and remaining oil together and drizzle over the salad. Divide among four plates and top with the olives, eggplant and fish. Drizzle a little of the cooking juices over each fish.

SERVES 4

Snapper pies

2 tablespoons olive oil
4 onions, thinly sliced
375 ml (13 fl oz/1½ cups) fish stock
875 ml (30 fl oz/3½ cups) pouring (whipping) cream
1 kg (2 lb 4 oz) skinless snapper fillets,
   cut into large pieces
2 sheets frozen puff pastry, thawed
1 egg, lightly beaten

Preheat the oven to 220°C (425°F/Gas 7). Heat the oil in a deep frying pan, add the onion and stir over medium heat for 20 minutes, or until the onion is slightly caramelized. Add the fish stock, bring to the boil and cook for 10 minutes, or until the liquid is nearly evaporated. Stir in the cream and bring to the boil. Reduce the heat and simmer for 20 minutes, or until the liquid is reduced by half.

Divide half the sauce among four 500 ml (17 fl oz/2 cup) ramekins. Place some fish pieces in each ramekin and top with the remaining sauce. Cut the pastry sheets slightly larger than the tops of the ramekins. Brush the edges of the pastry with a little of the egg, press the pastry onto the ramekins and brush the pastry top with the remaining beaten egg. Bake for 30 minutes, or until well puffed.

SERVES 4

Baked sea bass with wild rice stuffing

2 small fennel bulbs
4 tablespoons wild rice
250 ml (9 fl oz/1 cup) fish stock
40 g (1½ oz) butter
2 tablespoons olive oil
1 onion, chopped
1 garlic clove, crushed
grated zest of 1 lemon

1 whole sea bass, bass or any
  large white fish (about 2 kg/
  4 lb 8 oz), gutted and scaled
extra virgin olive oil
1 lemon, quartered
2 teaspoons chopped oregano
lemon wedges, to serve

Preheat the oven to 190°C (375°F/Gas 5) and lightly grease a large, shallow ovenproof dish. Thinly slice the fennel, reserving the green fronds.

Put the wild rice and stock in a saucepan with 3 tablespoons water and bring to the boil. Simmer for 30 minutes, or until tender, then drain. Heat the butter and olive oil in a large frying pan and gently cook the fennel, onion and garlic for 12–15 minutes, or until softened but not browned. Add the lemon zest, stir in the rice and season with salt and pepper.

Put the fish on a chopping board. Stuff the fish with a heaped tablespoon of the fennel mixture and a quarter of the reserved fennel fronds.

Spoon the remainder of the cooked fennel into the ovenproof dish and sprinkle with half the oregano. Put the fish on top of the fennel. Brush with extra virgin olive oil, squeeze over the lemon and season well. Sprinkle the remaining oregano over the fish and loosely cover the dish with foil. Bake for 25 minutes, or until it is just cooked through. Serve with lemon wedges.

SERVES 4

African fish bake

25 g (1 oz) butter, plus a little extra, for greasing the tin
2 onions, finely chopped
2 garlic cloves, crushed
2 tablespoons mild curry powder
½ teaspoon turmeric
grated zest and juice of 1 small lemon
100 g (3½ oz) raisins
4 tablespoons chopped blanched almonds
250 ml (9 fl oz/1 cup) milk
40 g (1½ oz) white bread
1 kg (2 lb 4 oz) skinless snook or cod fillet, finely chopped
2 large eggs

Preheat the oven to 190°C (375°F/Gas 5). Heat the butter in a frying pan and add the onion. Cook for 7–8 minutes, or until soft and lightly golden, stirring occasionally. Add the garlic and cook for a further 2 minutes. Mix in 1 tablespoon of the curry powder, the turmeric, lemon zest and juice, raisins and almonds. Remove from the heat and allow to cool for 10 minutes.

Pour 2½ tablespoons of the milk into a bowl and soak the bread in it for 10 minutes, turning over after 5 minutes. Squeeze the bread dry, then tear into small pieces and put in a bowl. Add the fish, one of the eggs and the mixture from the frying pan to the bowl, season well and mix together. Scoop into a lightly buttered non-stick 23 cm (9 inch) square tin that is 7 cm (2¾ inches) high. Bake for 15 minutes. Towards the end of the 15 minutes, whisk together the remaining milk, curry powder and egg. Pour the liquid over the top of the mixture in the tin. Bake for a further 45 minutes, or until set. Cool for 15 minutes, then cut into squares to serve.

SERVES 6

Baked prawn risotto with Thai flavours

300 ml (10½ fl oz) stock (fish, chicken or vegetable)
1 lemongrass stem, bruised
4 makrut (kaffir lime) leaves, finely shredded
2 tablespoons oil
1 small red onion, thinly sliced
1½–2 tablespoons Thai red curry paste
330 g (11½ oz/1½ cups) risotto rice
300 ml (10½ fl oz) coconut cream
600 g (1 lb 5 oz) raw medium prawns (shrimp),
    peeled and deveined, tails intact

Preheat the oven to 180°C (350°F/Gas 4). Pour the stock into a saucepan, add the lemongrass and half of the lime leaves. Bring to the boil then reduce the heat and simmer, covered, for 10 minutes.

Heat the oil in a flameproof casserole dish with a lid. Add the onion and cook over medium–low heat for 4–5 minutes, or until soft but not coloured. Stir in the curry paste and cook for a further minute, or until fragrant. Stir in the rice until well coated. Strain the stock into the rice then add the coconut cream. Cover and bake for 15 minutes.

Remove from the oven, stir the risotto well, then bake for a further 10–15 minutes. Add the prawns and mix them well into the rice — if the mixture looks a little dry add 125 ml (4 fl oz/½ cup) stock or water. Bake for a further 10–15 minutes, or until the prawns are cooked through and the rice is tender. Serve the risotto in bowls garnished with the remaining shredded lime leaves.

SERVES 4

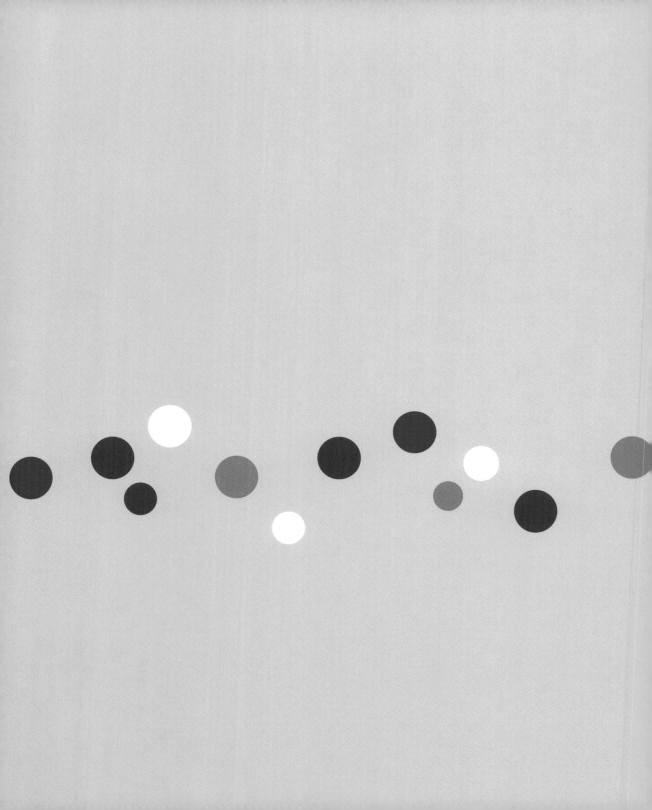

barbecue

Barbecued sardines with pesto

12 sardines, scaled and
  butterflied
250 ml (9 fl oz/1 cup) olive oil
1 tablespoon chopped rosemary
1 tablespoon chopped thyme
700 g (1 lb 9 oz) butternut
  pumpkin (squash)
2 small red onions

Pesto
3 large handfuls flat-leaf
  (Italian) parsley
2 garlic cloves
3 tablespoons macadamia nuts
90 g (3¼ oz/1 scant cup) grated
  parmesan cheese
150 ml (5 fl oz) olive oil

Pat the sardines dry and place in a non-metallic container. Season the fish on both sides with salt and pepper. Mix the oil with the rosemary and thyme and drizzle over the fish. Leave to marinate for an hour or so, or until you are ready to cook.

Meanwhile, slice the butternut pumpkin and cut into even-sized shapes measuring approximately 5 x 6 x 1 cm (2 x 2½ x ½ inches). Slice the onions in half widthways.

Make the pesto by putting all the ingredients in a food processor and whizzing to a paste. Alternatively, finely chop all the ingredients by hand and mix. Season to taste.

Lightly oil a barbecue flat plate and heat it to high direct heat. Cook the pumpkin, onion and fish for 2–3 minutes on each side, brushing regularly with the remaining herb oil. You will need a spatula to turn the pumpkin on the barbecue. Serve each person three sardines on a small bed of pumpkin slices with half a red onion and a generous spoonful of pesto.

SERVES 4

Piri piri prawns

1 kg (2 lb 4 oz) raw large
  prawns (shrimp)
4 long red chillies, seeded
185 ml (6 fl oz/¾ cup) white
  wine vinegar

2 large garlic cloves, chopped
6–8 small red chillies, chopped
125 ml (4 fl oz/½ cup) olive oil
150 g (5½ oz) mixed lettuce
  leaves

Remove the heads from the prawns and slice them down the back without cutting right through, leaving the tail intact. Open out each prawn and remove the dark vein, then store the prepared prawns in the fridge while you make the sauce.

To make the sauce, put the long chillies in a saucepan with the vinegar and simmer over medium–high heat for 5 minutes, or until the chillies are soft. Let the mixture cool slightly, then put the chillies and 3 tablespoons of the vinegar in a food processor. Add the garlic and chopped small chillies and blend until the mixture is smooth. While the motor is running, gradually add the oil and remaining vinegar to the food processor.

Put the prawns in the marinade, making sure they are well coated, then cover them and refrigerate for 30 minutes.

Take the prawns out of the marinade, bring the marinade to the boil and let it simmer for 5 minutes, or until it is slightly thickened and reduced. Take the prawns and the marinade out to the barbecue, and leave the saucepan with the marinade in it on the edge of the barbecue to keep warm.

Lightly oil the barbecue chargrill plate and heat it to high direct heat. Cook the prawns, basting them with the marinade, for 2–3 minutes on each side, or until they are cooked through. Arrange the lettuce on four plates, top with the prawns and serve immediately with the chilli sauce.

SERVES 4

Involtini

1 kg (2 lb 4 oz) skinless firm white fish fillets, cut into 4 x 5 cm (1½ x 2 inch) pieces	4 tablespoons finely grated parmesan cheese
3 lemons	120 g (4¼ oz/1½ cups) fresh breadcrumbs
4 tablespoons olive oil	2 tablespoons chopped flat-leaf (Italian) parsley
1 small onion, chopped	1 egg, lightly beaten
3 garlic cloves, chopped	24 bay leaves
2 tablespoons chopped capers	2 small white onions, quartered and separated into pieces
2 tablespoons chopped pitted Kalamata olives	2 tablespoons lemon juice, extra

Cut each fish piece horizontally in half — you should get 16 thin slices. Place each slice between two pieces of plastic wrap and roll gently with a rolling pin to flatten without tearing. Cut each piece in half to give 32 pieces. Peel the lemons with a vegetable peeler. Cut the peel into 24 even pieces. Squeeze the lemons to give 3 tablespoons of juice.

Heat 2 tablespoons of the olive oil in a pan, add the onion and garlic, and cook over medium heat for 2 minutes. Place in a bowl with the capers, olives, parmesan, breadcrumbs and parsley. Season, add the egg and mix to bind.

Divide the stuffing among the fish pieces and, with oiled hands, roll up to form parcels. Thread the rolls onto eight skewers, four rolls per skewer, alternating with the bay leaves, lemon peel and onion.

Mix the remaining oil with the lemon juice. Lightly oil a barbecue flat plate and heat it to high direct heat. Cook the skewers for 3–4 minutes each side, basting with the oil and lemon mixture. Drizzle with a little extra lemon juice, then serve.

SERVES 4

Vietnamese fish

1 whole small, firm white fish
    (about 750 g/1 lb 10 oz),
    gutted and scaled
2 teaspoons green peppercorns,
    finely crushed
2 teaspoons chopped red chilli
3 teaspoons fish sauce
2 teaspoons oil
1 tablespoon oil, extra
2 onions, thinly sliced
4 cm (1½ inch) piece fresh
    ginger, thinly sliced
3 garlic cloves, thinly sliced

2 teaspoons sugar
4 spring onions (scallions), cut
    into short lengths, then finely
    shredded

**Lemon and garlic
dipping sauce**
3 tablespoons lemon juice
2 tablespoons fish sauce
1 tablespoon sugar
2 small red chillies, chopped
3 garlic cloves, crushed

Cut two diagonal slashes in the thickest part of the fish on both sides. In a food processor or mortar and pestle, grind the peppercorns, chilli and fish sauce to a paste and brush over the fish. Leave for 20 minutes.

To make the dipping sauce, mix together all the ingredients.

Lightly oil a barbecue chargrill plate and heat it to high direct heat. Cook the fish for 8 minutes on each side, or until the flesh flakes easily when tested.

While the fish is cooking, heat the extra oil in a pan and cook the onion over medium heat, stirring, until golden. Add the ginger, garlic and sugar and cook for 3 minutes. Place the fish on a serving plate, top with the onion mixture and sprinkle with spring onion. Serve with the dipping sauce.

SERVES 6

Marinated and seared tuna

4 tablespoons soy sauce
3 tablespoons mirin
1 tablespoon sake
1 teaspoon caster (superfine) sugar
1 teaspoon finely grated fresh ginger
2 teaspoons lemon juice
4 x 175 g (6 oz) tuna steaks
1 tablespoon oil
coriander (cilantro) leaves, to garnish

Mix the soy sauce, mirin, sake, sugar, ginger and lemon juice together in a bowl. Put the tuna steaks in a shallow dish and spoon the marinade over the top. Turn the fish in the marinade, ensuring it is well coated. Cover and leave to marinate for 30 minutes in the fridge.

Lift the tuna out of the marinade and pour the marinade into a small saucepan. Bring the marinade to the boil and reduce for 1 minute.

Meanwhile, lightly oil a barbecue chargrill plate and heat it to high direct heat. Cook the tuna steaks for 2–3 minutes on each side so that the tuna is cooked on the outside but still pink in the middle. Serve with some of the marinade spooned over the top and garnished with coriander. Serve with rice and steamed vegetables.

SERVES 4

Miso-glazed salmon and eggplant salad

5 tablespoons sesame seeds, lightly toasted
3 tablespoons white miso paste
1 tablespoon sake
1 tablespoon mirin
1 tablespoon sugar
3 tablespoons dashi stock
1 large eggplant (aubergine), cut into 1 cm (½ inch) rounds
2 garlic cloves, crushed
3 tablespoons olive oil
2 teaspoons dark soy sauce
3 tablespoons dashi stock, extra
1 teaspoon sugar, extra
1 teaspoon grated fresh ginger
150 g (5½ oz) snowpea (mangetout) shoots
400 g (14 oz) daikon, cut into matchsticks
4 skinless salmon fillets

To make the glaze, put the sesame seeds in a spice grinder or mortar and pestle and grind until they have a rough, flaky texture. Whisk the miso, sake, mirin, sugar and dashi stock together until smooth and stir in half of the crushed sesame seeds.

Put the eggplant in a large bowl with the combined garlic and oil and toss well.

To make the dressing, whisk together the soy sauce, extra dashi and sugar, ginger and remaining crushed sesame seeds. Put the snowpea shoots and daikon in a large bowl, add the dressing and toss well. Cover and refrigerate until needed.

Lightly oil a barbecue flat plate and heat it to medium–high direct heat. Cook the eggplant for 3–4 minutes on each side, or until soft, then cut into quarters. Brush both sides of each salmon fillet with the glaze and cook for 2 minutes each side, or until almost cooked through, brushing with the glaze midway. Flake the fish with a fork and toss through the salad with the eggplant. Season and serve.

SERVES 4

Cajun swordfish

1 tablespoon garlic powder
1 tablespoon onion powder
2 teaspoons white pepper
2 teaspoons cracked black pepper
2 teaspoons dried thyme
2 teaspoons dried oregano
1 teaspoon cayenne pepper
4 x 200 g (7 oz) swordfish steaks
oil, for cooking
lime wedges, to serve
Greek-style yoghurt, to serve

Mix all the dried spices and herbs in a bowl. Pat the swordfish steaks dry with paper towels, then coat both sides of each steak in the spice mixture, shaking off any excess.

Lightly oil a barbecue flat plate and heat it to high direct heat. Cook the swordfish steaks for 3–5 minutes on each side, depending on the thickness of each steak. Serve with wedges of lime, a dollop of yoghurt and a mixed leaf salad.

SERVES 4

Rosemary tuna kebabs

3 tomatoes
1 tablespoon olive oil
2–3 small red chillies, seeded
   and chopped
3–4 garlic cloves, crushed
1 red onion, finely chopped
3 tablespoons dry white wine
   or water
400 g (14 oz) tin chickpeas,
   rinsed
3 tablespoons chopped oregano

4 tablespoons chopped flat-leaf
   (Italian) parsley
lemon wedges, to serve

Tuna kebabs
1 kg (2 lb 4 oz) piece of tuna,
   cut into 4 cm (1½ inch) cubes
8 rosemary stems, about 20 cm
   (8 inches) long, with the
   leaves from the stem thinned
   out a little
cooking oil spray

Cut the tomatoes into halves or quarters and use a teaspoon to scrape out the seeds. Roughly chop the flesh.

Heat the oil in a large non-stick frying pan. Add the chilli, garlic and onion and stir over medium heat for 5 minutes, or until softened. Add the chopped tomato and the wine or water. Cook over low heat for 10 minutes, or until the mixture is soft and pulpy and most of the liquid has evaporated. Stir in the chickpeas with the oregano and parsley. Season to taste with salt and freshly ground black pepper.

Lightly oil a barbecue flat plate and heat it to high direct heat. Thread the tuna onto the rosemary stems, lightly spray with oil, then cook, turning, for 3 minutes, or until lightly browned on the outside but still a little pink in the centre. Serve with the chickpea salad and some lemon wedges.

SERVES 4

Snapper envelope with ginger and spring onions

Dressing
1 spring onion (scallion)
3 tablespoons coriander (cilantro) leaves
1 teaspoon finely grated fresh ginger
2 tablespoons lime juice
1 tablespoon fish sauce
½ teaspoon sesame oil

1 whole snapper (about 1.8–2 kg/4 lb–4 lb 8 oz), cleaned
1 lime
4 spring onions (scallions)
3 large handfuls coriander (cilantro) leaves
1 tablespoon finely grated fresh ginger
cooking oil spray

To make the dressing, thinly slice the green part of the spring onion and the coriander leaves, and mix with the ginger, lime juice, fish sauce and sesame oil.

Use a sharp knife to score the fish flesh in a diamond pattern. Lightly season.

Peel the lime, removing all the pith, and separate the lime sections by cutting each piece away from the membrane. Slice the spring onions on the diagonal, then mix with the coriander, lime segments and ginger. Stuff the mixture into the fish cavity.

Preheat a kettle or covered barbecue to medium indirect heat. Lightly spray a double layer of foil with oil. Fold the foil around the fish and seal the edges tightly. Put the fish in the middle of the barbecue and cook it, covered, for 10 minutes. Use a large metal spatula to turn the fish over and cook for another 8–10 minutes, or until it flakes when tested in the thickest part of the flesh. Open the foil envelope and slide the fish onto a serving plate. Pour the cooking juices over the fish, drizzle the dressing over the top and serve straight away.

SERVES 4

Smoked trout with lemon and dill butter

Lemon and dill butter
125 g (4½ oz) butter, softened
2 tablespoons lemon juice
2 tablespoons finely chopped dill
½ teaspoon lemon zest
1 small garlic clove, crushed

6 hickory woodchips (see Note)
4 whole rainbow trout, gutted
    and scaled
oil, for brushing

Mash together the butter, lemon juice, dill, zest and garlic, shape it into a log and wrap it in baking paper, twisting the ends to seal. Refrigerate the butter until it is firm, then cut it into 1 cm (½ inch) thick slices and leave it at room temperature.

Preheat a kettle barbecue to low indirect heat, allow the coals to burn down to ash, then add three hickory woodchips to each side.

Brush the skin of the fish with oil. When the woodchips begin to smoke, put the trout on the barbecue, replace the cover and smoke them for 15 minutes or until they are cooked through. Remove the fish from the grill, gently peel off the skin and top them with the lemon and dill butter while they are still hot. Smoked trout are delicious with boiled new potatoes and a green salad, and can also be served cold.

SERVES 4

NOTE: Special woodchips are commercially available which will give off a wonderfully scented smoke and infuse your food with a distinctive flavour — in this recipe we use hickory woodchips. Never use wood that is not specifically intended for smoking food, as many woods are chemically treated and may make the food poisonous. Smoking does not work in a gas or electric barbecue as the chips need to burn to release their aromatic flavour.

Herbed scampi with sweet cider sauce

16 scampi or moreton bay bugs (flat-head lobster)
4 tablespoons olive oil
150 ml (5 fl oz) lemon juice
3 garlic cloves, crushed
1 large handful flat-leaf (Italian) parsley, finely chopped
3 tablespoons finely chopped dill, plus some extra, to garnish
4 tablespoons apple cider
40 g (1½ oz) butter

Remove the heads from the scampi, then cut them in half lengthways. Place in a single layer in a shallow non-metallic dish. Combine the olive oil, lemon juice, garlic, parsley and dill and pour over the scampi. Cover and refrigerate for at least 1 hour.

Lightly oil a barbecue chargrill plate and heat it to high direct heat. Cook the scampi, shell-side down, for 2 minutes. Turn and cook for another 2 minutes, or until tender. Transfer to a serving platter.

Simmer the apple cider in a small saucepan until reduced by two-thirds. Reduce the heat and add the butter, stirring until melted. Remove from the heat, pour over the scampi and serve. Serve with crusty bread and a green salad.

SERVES 4

Squid with picada dressing

500 g (1 lb 2 oz) small squid

Picada dressing
2 tablespoons extra virgin olive oil
2 tablespoons flat-leaf (Italian) parsley,
   finely chopped
1 garlic clove, crushed
¼ teaspoon cracked black pepper

To clean the squid, gently pull the tentacles away from the tube (the intestines should come away at the same time). Remove the intestines from the tentacles by cutting under the eyes, then remove the beak, if it remains in the centre of the tentacles, by pushing up with your index finger. Pull away the soft bone.

Rub the tubes under cold running water and the skin should come away easily. Wash the tubes and tentacles and drain well. Put in a bowl, with ¼ teaspoon salt and mix well. Cover and refrigerate for about 30 minutes.

For the picada dressing, whisk together the olive oil, parsley, garlic, cracked black pepper and some salt.

Lightly oil a barbecue chargrill plate and heat it to high direct heat. Cook the squid tubes in small batches for 2–3 minutes, or until white and tender. Barbecue or grill the squid tentacles, turning to brown them all over, for 1 minute, or until they curl up. Serve hot, drizzled with the picada dressing.

SERVES 6 AS A STARTER

Teriyaki baby octopus

125 ml (4 fl oz/½ cup) sake
125 ml (4 fl oz/½ cup) mirin
125 ml (4 fl oz/½ cup) dark soy
    sauce
1 tablespoon caster (superfine)
    sugar

2 teaspoons grated fresh ginger
2 garlic cloves, finely chopped
1 kg (2 lb 4 oz) baby octopus

Combine the sake, mirin, dark soy sauce and sugar in a small saucepan. Bring the mixture to the boil over medium heat and boil, stirring until all the sugar has dissolved, then add the ginger and garlic and remove the saucepan from the heat. Leave the mixture to cool for 30 minutes.

To prepare the octopus, use a small knife to carefully cut between the head and tentacles of the octopus, just below the eyes. Grasp the body and push the beak out and up through the tentacles with your fingers. Cut the eyes from the head by slicing off a small disc. Discard the eye section. Carefully slit through one side, avoiding the ink sac, and scrape out any gut. Rinse the octopus well under running water. Cut it in half. Wash the rest of the octopus thoroughly under running water, pulling the skin away from the tube and tentacles. If the octopus are large, cut the tentacles into quarters.

Put the octopus in a large, non-metallic bowl. Whisk the teriyaki marinade, making sure that it is well combined, then pour it over the octopus, stirring so that the octopus is thoroughly coated. Cover and marinate it in the fridge for at least 2 hours, or overnight if time permits.

Lightly oil a barbecue chargrill plate and heat to medium direct heat. Remove the octopus from the teriyaki marinade and cook them for 2–3 minutes, or until they are cooked through, curled and glazed. Serve on a bed of Asian salad.

SERVES 4

Fresh tuna Niçoise

4 eggs
600 g (1 lb 5 oz) boiling potatoes
200 g (7 oz) green beans
700 g (1 lb 9 oz) tuna steaks, about 2 cm (¾ inch) thick
90 ml (3 fl oz) olive oil
2 tablespoons red wine vinegar
2 tablespoons chopped flat-leaf (Italian) parsley
20 cherry tomatoes, halved
1 small red onion, thinly sliced
100 g (3½ oz/¾ cup) pitted black olives

Place the eggs in a saucepan of cold water, bring to the boil, then reduce the heat and simmer for 4 minutes. Cool the eggs under cold running water, then shell and quarter.

Return the water to the boil, add the potatoes, then reduce the heat and simmer for 12 minutes, or until tender. Remove and set aside. Add the beans to the pan and cook for 3–4 minutes, or until tender but still bright green. Drain, refresh under cold water and halve. Slice the potatoes thickly.

Lightly oil a barbecue chargrill plate and heat it to high direct heat. Rub pepper on both sides of the tuna. Cook for 2 minutes on each side for rare, or until still pink in the middle. Cool slightly, then slice.

Combine the oil, vinegar and parsley in a small cup. Gently toss the potato, beans, tomatoes, onion and olives in a bowl, and season. Add three-quarters of the dressing and toss well. Divide among four bowls, top with the tuna and egg, and drizzle with the remaining dressing.

SERVES 4

Scallops with sesame bok choy

2 tablespoons light soy sauce
1 tablespoon fish sauce
1 tablespoon honey
1 tablespoon kecap manis (see
   Note)
grated zest and juice of 1 lime
2 teaspoons grated fresh ginger
24 large scallops, with roe,
   membrane removed
lime wedges, to serve

Sesame bok choy
1 tablespoon sesame oil
1 tablespoon sesame seeds
1 garlic clove, crushed
8 baby bok choy (pak choy),
   halved lengthways

Mix the soy and fish sauces, honey, kecap manis, lime zest and juice and ginger.
Pour over the scallops, cover and refrigerate for 15 minutes. Drain, reserving the
marinade. Lightly oil a barbecue flat plate and heat it to high direct heat.

To make the sesame bok choy, pour the oil onto the hot barbecue flat plate and add
the sesame seeds and garlic. Cook, stirring, for 1 minute, or until the seeds are
golden. Arrange the bok choy in a single layer on the hot plate and pour over the
reserved marinade. Cook for 3–4 minutes, turning once, until tender. Remove from
the barbecue and keep warm.

Wipe clean the flat plate, brush with oil and reheat. Add the scallops and cook, turning,
for about 2 minutes, or until they become opaque. Serve on top of the bok choy,
with the lime wedges.

SERVES 4

NOTE: Instead of kecap manis, you can use soy sauce sweetened with a little soft
brown sugar.

Sweet and sour fish kebabs

750 g (1 lb 10 oz) skinless thick ling or cod fillets
225 g (8 oz) tin pineapple pieces
1 large red capsicum (pepper)
1 tablespoon soy sauce
1½ tablespoons soft brown sugar
2 tablespoons white vinegar
2 tablespoons tomato sauce

Soak 12 wooden skewers in cold water for 30 minutes. This is to ensure they don't burn during cooking. Meanwhile, cut the fish into 2.5 cm (1 inch) cubes. Drain the pineapple, reserving 2 tablespoons of liquid. Cut the capsicum into 2.5 cm (1 inch) pieces. Thread the capsicum, fish and pineapple alternately onto the skewers.

Place the kebabs in a shallow non-metallic dish. Combine the soy sauce, reserved pineapple juice, sugar, vinegar and tomato sauce in a small bowl. Mix well and pour over the kebabs. Cover and refrigerate for 2–3 hours.

Lightly oil a barbecue chargrill plate and heat it to high direct heat. Cook the kebabs, brushing frequently with the marinade, for 2–3 minutes each side, or until just cooked through. Serve immediately with a simple green salad.

MAKES 12 SKEWERS

Redfish in corn husks with asparagus and red capsicum salad

Salad
1 red capsicum (pepper)
2 tablespoons virgin olive oil
1 small garlic clove, crushed
1 tablespoon lemon juice
1 tablespoon chopped basil
1 tablespoon pine nuts
100 g (3½ oz/½ cup) small black
  olives

6 whole small red mullet,
  gutted and scaled
12 lemon thyme sprigs
1 lemon, sliced
2 garlic cloves, sliced
12 large corn husks
olive oil, for drizzling
18 asparagus spears, trimmed
lemon wedges, to serve

Preheat a kettle or covered barbecue to medium indirect heat. To make the salad, cut the capsicum into large pieces. Hold over the coals or gas flame of a barbecue until charred all over. Cool in a plastic bag, then peel off the skin. Finely dice the flesh. Combine the olive oil, garlic, lemon juice and basil in a small bowl and whisk together. Add the capsicum, pine nuts and olives.

Wash the fish and pat dry inside and out with paper towels. Fill each fish cavity with thyme, lemon and garlic, then place each fish in a corn husk. Drizzle with oil and sprinkle with pepper, then top each fish with another husk. Tie the ends closed.

Place on coals or on a barbecue and cook, turning once, for 6–8 minutes, or until the fish is cooked and flakes easily when tested with a fork. A few minutes after you've started cooking the fish, brush the asparagus with oil and cook on the barbecue. Pour the dressing over the asparagus and serve with the fish and salad.

SERVES 6

Barbecued chermoula prawns

1 kg (2 lb 4 oz) raw medium
    prawns (shrimp)
3 teaspoons hot paprika
2 teaspoons ground cumin
3 large handfuls flat-leaf
    (Italian) parsley
1 large handful coriander
    (cilantro) leaves

100 ml (3½ fl oz) lemon juice
145 ml (4¾ fl oz) olive oil
280 g (10 oz/1½ cups) couscous
1 tablespoon grated lemon zest
lemon wedges, to serve

Peel the prawns, leaving the tails intact. Gently pull out the dark vein from the backs, starting at the head end. Place the prawns in a large bowl. Dry-fry the paprika and cumin in a frying pan for about 1 minute, or until fragrant. Remove from the heat.

Blend or process the spices, parsley, coriander, lemon juice and 125 ml (4 fl oz/½ cup) of the oil until finely chopped. Add a little salt and pepper. Pour over the prawns and mix well, then cover with plastic wrap and refrigerate for 10 minutes.

Meanwhile, to cook the couscous, bring 250 ml (9 fl oz/1 cup) water to the boil in a saucepan, then stir in the couscous, lemon zest, the remaining oil and ¼ teaspoon salt. Remove from the heat, cover and leave for 5 minutes. Fluff the couscous with a fork, adding a little extra olive oil if needed.

Lightly oil a barbecue chargrill plate and heat it to high direct heat. Cook the prawns for 3–4 minutes, or until cooked through, turning and brushing with extra marinade while cooking (take care not to overcook). Serve the prawns on a bed of couscous, with a wedge of lemon.

SERVES 4

Tuna steaks with salsa and garlic mash

Garlic mash

1 kg (2 lb 4 oz) boiling potatoes,
   cut into chunks
6–8 garlic cloves
4 tablespoons milk
3 tablespoons olive oil

Salsa

1 tablespoon olive oil
2 French shallots, finely chopped
200 g (7 oz) green olives, pitted
   and quartered lengthways

3 tablespoons currants, soaked
   in warm water for 10 minutes
1 tablespoon baby capers,
   rinsed and squeezed dry
1 tablespoon sherry vinegar
2 tablespoons shredded mint

4 x 150 g (5½ oz) tuna steaks
olive oil, for brushing

Boil the potato and garlic for 10–15 minutes, or until tender. Drain, then return the pan to the heat to evaporate any excess water. Remove the pan from the heat and mash the potato and garlic until smooth, then stir in the milk and oil, and season.

To make the salsa, heat the oil in a frying pan over medium heat. Cook the shallots for 2–4 minutes, or until soft but not browned, then add the olives, drained currants and capers. Cook for 2 minutes, stirring continuously, then add the vinegar and cook for 2 minutes, or until the liquid is reduced by about half. Remove the pan from the heat and keep the salsa warm until you're ready to dish up.

Lightly oil a barbecue chargrill plate and heat it to medium–high direct heat. Brush the tuna steaks with olive oil, season them well and cook for 2–3 minutes each side for medium–rare, or until they are cooked to your liking. Stir the mint into the salsa and serve it immediately with the garlic mash and tuna.

SERVES 4

Barbecued sweet chilli seafood on banana mats

500 g (1 lb 2 oz) raw medium prawns (shrimp), peeled and
   deveined, tails intact
300 g (10½ oz) scallops, without roe, membrane removed
500 g (1 lb 2 oz) baby squid, cleaned and tubes quartered
500 g (1 lb 2 oz) baby octopus, cleaned
250 ml (9 fl oz/1 cup) sweet chilli sauce
1 tablespoon fish sauce
2 tablespoons lime juice
3 tablespoons vegetable oil
banana leaves, cut into squares, to serve
lime wedges, to serve

Place the prawns, scallops, squid and the octopus in a shallow, non-metallic bowl.

In a separate bowl combine the sweet chilli sauce, fish sauce, lime juice and
1 tablespoon of the vegetable oil. Pour the mixture over the seafood and mix gently to
coat. Allow to marinate for 1 hour. Drain the seafood well and reserve the marinade.

Heat the remaining oil on a barbecue flat plate and heat it to high direct heat. Cook
the seafood in batches (depending on the size of your barbecue) for 3–5 minutes, or
until tender. Drizzle each batch with a little of the leftover marinade during cooking.

Pile the seafood high onto the squares of banana leaf and serve with wedges of lime.

SERVES 4

Prawn skewers with coconut sambal

4 tablespoons coconut cream
3 tablespoons lime juice
2 tablespoons soy sauce
1 tablespoon grated lime zest
2 teaspoons chopped red chilli
1 teaspoon grated palm sugar
   (jaggery) or soft brown sugar
½ teaspoon shrimp paste
4 garlic cloves, crushed
32 raw medium prawns
   (shrimp), peeled and
   deveined, tails intact
2 teaspoons oil

1 tablespoon chopped coriander
   (cilantro)
mango chutney

Coconut sambal

3 tablespoons desiccated
   coconut
3 tablespoons sesame seeds
½ teaspoon dried garlic flakes
¼ teaspoon ground coriander
¼ teaspoon ground cumin
3 tablespoons toasted unsalted
   peanuts, roughly chopped

Soak eight bamboo skewers in water for 30 minutes. To make the marinade, combine the coconut cream, lime juice, soy sauce, lime zest, chilli, sugar, shrimp paste and garlic and mix until the sugar dissolves. Thread four prawns onto each skewer. Place on a non-metallic plate, cover with the marinade and refrigerate for 1 hour.

To make the sambal, toast the coconut in a dry frying pan for 1–2 minutes, or until golden, then add the sesame seeds, garlic flakes, spices and ½ teaspoon salt and cook briefly. Remove from the heat and stir in the peanuts.

Lightly oil a barbecue chargrill plate and heat it to high direct heat. Cook the prawns on both sides for 2–3 minutes, or until pink and cooked. Place on a platter and sprinkle with coriander. Serve with the sambal and chutney.

SERVES 4

Swordfish with anchovy and caper sauce

Sauce
1 large garlic clove
1 tablespoon capers, rinsed and finely chopped
50 g (1¾ oz) anchovy fillets, finely chopped
1 tablespoon finely chopped rosemary or dried oregano
finely grated zest and juice of ½ lemon
4 tablespoons extra virgin olive oil
1 large tomato, finely chopped

4 x 200 g (7 oz) swordfish steaks
1 tablespoon extra virgin olive oil
crusty Italian bread, to serve

Put the garlic in a mortar and pestle with a little salt and crush it. To make the sauce, mix together the garlic, capers, anchovies, rosemary or oregano, lemon zest and juice, oil and tomato. Leave for 10 minutes.

Preheat a barbecue grill or chargrill pan to very hot. Using paper towels, pat the swordfish dry and lightly brush with the olive oil. Season with salt and pepper. Sear the swordfish over high heat for about 2 minutes on each side (depending on the thickness of the steaks), or until just cooked. The best way to check if the fish is cooked is to pull apart the centre of one steak — the flesh should be opaque. (Serve with the cut side underneath.)

If the cooked swordfish is a little oily, drain it on paper towels, then place on serving plates and drizzle with the sauce. Serve with Italian bread to mop up the sauce.

SERVES 4

index

First published in 2009 by Murdoch Books Pty Limited

Murdoch Books Australia
Pier 8/9, 23 Hickson Road
Millers Point NSW 2000
Phone: +61 (0) 2 8220 2000
Fax: +61 (0) 2 8220 2558
www.murdochbooks.com.au

Murdoch Books UK Limited
Erico House, 6th Floor
93–99 Upper Richmond Road
Putney, London SW15 2TG
Phone: +44 (0) 20 8785 5995
Fax: +44 (0) 20 8785 5985
www.murdochbooks.co.uk

Chief Executive: Juliet Rogers
Publishing Director: Kay Scarlett

Design manager: Vivien Valk
Project manager: Gordana Trifunovic
Editor: Zoë Harpham
Design concept: Alex Frampton
Designer: Susanne Geppert
Production: Kita George
Cover photography: Michele Aboud
Cover styling: Sarah De Nardi
Recipes developed by the Murdoch Books Test Kitchen

Printed by Sing Cheong Printing Co. Ltd in 2009. PRINTED IN HONG KONG.

National Library of Australia Cataloguing-in-Publication Data
    Fish. Includes index.
    ISBN 978 1 74196 346 5 (pbk).
    1. Cookery (Fish) 2. Cookery (Seafood) (Series: Test kitchen) 641.692

IMPORTANT: Those who might be at risk from the effects of salmonella poisoning (the
elderly, pregnant women, young children and those suffering from immune deficiency
diseases) should consult their doctor with any concerns about eating raw eggs.

CONVERSION GUIDE: You may find cooking times vary depending on the oven you
are using. For fan-forced ovens, as a general rule, set the oven temperature to 20°C
(35°F) lower than indicated in the recipe. We have used 20 ml (4 teaspoon) tablespoon
measures. If you are using a 15 ml (3 teaspoon) tablespoon, for most recipes the
difference will not be noticeable. However, for recipes using baking powder, gelatine,
bicarbonate of soda (baking soda), small amounts of flour and cornflour (cornstarch),
add an extra teaspoon for each tablespoon specified.